USED / REUSED

BY FELIPE GALINDO FEGGO

The exhibition
PORTRAITS OF MY COMMUNITY
by Felipe Galindo Feggo
at the Morris-Jumel Mansion, New York City
October 7, 2021 - January 2, 2022
is made possible in part with funding from
the Upper Manhattan Empowerment Zone Development Corporation
and administered by the Lower Manhattan Cultural Council.

The companion book
USED/REUSED
is made possible in part with a grant from
the Northern Manhattan Business Association Program,
a collaboration between the Hispanic Federation, Northern Manhattan Arts Alliance,
The Miranda Family and Google.

For more on the work of Felipe Galindo,
please visit felipegalindo.com

Edited & Designed by Martin Kozlowski,
please visit martinkozlowski.com

For more on Now What Media Books,
please visit nowwhatmedia.com/nowwhatbooks.html

This book may be purchased in bulk for promotional, educational or business purposes.
Please contact editor @ nowwhatmedia.com

Cover Image: "Roasted Ducks III", mixed media on Chinese food container.

Introduction

The Art of Felipe Galindo

New York's art world had reached an interesting point when Felipe Galindo arrived on the scene in the early Eighties. Only a couple decades earlier Pop Art had opened the gates for the adventurous artist, announcing that anything was possible. For an artist in possession of the right sensibility, boundaries were illusions—inconvenient structures symptomatic of a failed imagination. Art was, in fact, in the process of re-imagined, re-contextualized, re-represented, and in some cases re-packaged. Total originality—always a difficult if not an impossible feat—seemed to become particularly demanding. But the dedicated few strove for it just the same. "Neo" became a familiar prefix, attaching itself to everything from Expressionism to Pop. Some called the new wave Graffiti Art.

Not everyone was caught up in the rage to categorize. Some, like Galindo, preferred the more challenging course of making art. Mixed media seemed to flow naturally from his beginnings as an illustrator and cartoonist, as well as his natural impulses as an artist, and it made possible startling juxtapositions. It seemed a perfect strategy for artists straddling a cultural divide. The collagic dimension of his work makes use of newspapers, coffee cups, menus, etc.—anything that might be re-purposed in order to rearrange and extend aesthetic priorities. In his work, thematic tensions coexist and are resolved with a beguiling ease. The ideas of transit and stillness are omnipresent—sometimes within the same painting. Not surprising in an artist who counts among his influence, Felipe Galindo's commitment to figurative representation remains at the core of his art. The scenes are diverse, democratic, unexpected, reflecting the artist's methods of depiction. His work reflects urban life in all of its variousness and self-contradictions. In Galindo's world strangers press against one another as they navigate the world in close proximity, on city streets, in shops, on subway platforms where they stand like unwitting actors in an age-old play, inching their way toward a fateful precipice.

C.S. Ledbetter
Associate Editor
The New Yorker

USED / REUSED

I began to create artworks for my *Used/Reused* series in 1983, a few months after arriving in New York, from my native Mexico. As a new immigrant, I was in awe of the diversity of packaged food available, and I was shocked by the amount of waste that this generated. I was attracted by the graphic qualities of these disposable materials, so I began collecting interesting paper bags, boxes, cans, labels, cartons and food containers, and began to create artworks that would transform these symbols of consumerism.

I was interested in exploring the materials and also the concept of longevity. I find some irony in the fact that we as artists are concerned with the longevity of our materials, yet a plastic bag will take 1000 years to decompose in a landfill. I began this series using discarded materials to create personal works for gallery and museum exhibitions, separate from my cartoon and illustration art. This particular body of work allows me to experiment and play freely, without the pressure of an assignment, and it honors and parodies my art school years, when I learned to make "serious" art.

In the spring of 1987 I got an illustration assignment from the late art director Wes Anderson for an essay by Jim Mullen, to be published in *The Village Voice*. The satirical piece was about classic New York Greek diners, which I was fascinated by since my arrival in the city, when I used to spend hours in a corner booth (during no-peak hours,) drinking coffee, observing people and drawing. The concept of "coffee to go" seemed still foreign to me, but the paper cups were visually interesting… and very New York. I integrated a flattened paper cup for that assignment. The only other job I ever did using discarded materials was for *The New York Times* a few years ago.

These Used/Reused artworks spring from observation, as I depict everyday life situations while expressing my impressions of society and creating visual commentaries that are slightly humorous or slightly tragic. The series is also informed by my practice of compulsive sketching, and my ever-growing collection of sketchbooks provides an endless source of material.

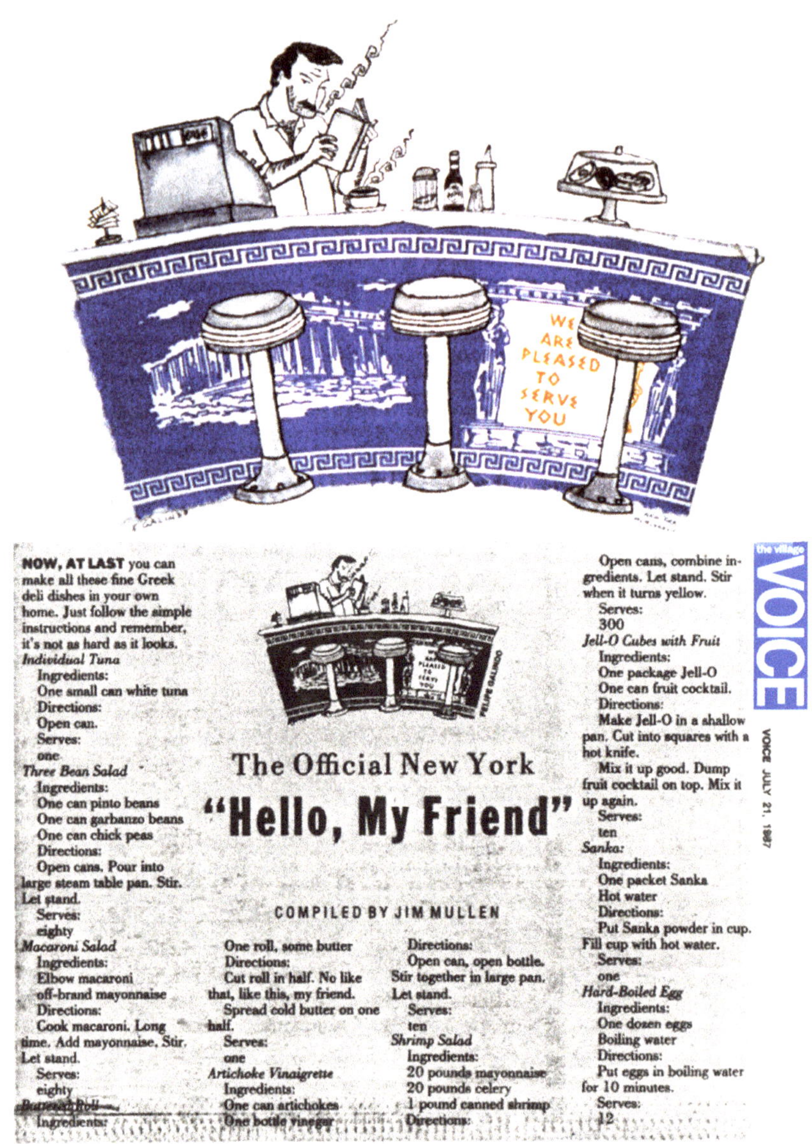

The Official New York

"Hello, My Friend"

COMPILED BY JIM MULLEN

NOW, AT LAST you can make all these fine Greek deli dishes in your own home. Just follow the simple instructions and remember, it's not as hard as it looks.

Individual Tuna
Ingredients:
One small can white tuna
Directions:
Open can.
Serves:
one

Three Bean Salad
Ingredients:
One can pinto beans
One can garbanzo beans
One can chick peas
Directions:
Open cans. Pour into large steam table pan. Stir. Let stand.
Serves:
eighty

Macaroni Salad
Ingredients:
Elbow macaroni
off-brand mayonnaise
Directions:
Cook macaroni. Long time. Add mayonnaise. Stir. Let stand.
Serves:
eighty

Buttered Roll
Ingredients:
One roll, some butter
Directions:
Cut roll in half. No like that, like this, my friend.
Spread cold butter on one half.
Serves:
one

Artichoke Vinaigrette
Ingredients:
One can artichokes
One bottle vinegar
Directions:
Open can, open bottle. Stir together in large pan. Let stand.
Serves:
ten

Shrimp Salad
Ingredients:
20 pounds mayonnaise
20 pounds celery
1 pound canned shrimp
Directions:
Open cans, combine ingredients. Let stand. Stir when it turns yellow.
Serves:
300

Jell-O Cubes with Fruit
Ingredients:
One package Jell-O
One can fruit cocktail.
Directions:
Make Jell-O in a shallow pan. Cut into squares with a hot knife.
Mix it up good. Dump fruit cocktail on top. Mix it up again.
Serves:
ten

Sanka:
Ingredients:
One packet Sanka
Hot water
Directions:
Put Sanka powder in cup. Fill cup with hot water.
Serves:
one

Hard-Boiled Egg
Ingredients:
One dozen eggs
Boiling water
Directions:
Put eggs in boiling water for 10 minutes.
Serves:
12

The works are created in mixed media, mixing various materials, including watercolor, pastel, inks, acrylics, and collage. Sometimes I also sketch directly on the objects, especially when inspiration strikes while I'm on the subway, bus, restaurant or at an event. Different kinds of objects, like paper bags, coffee cups, cans, maps, and all sorts of containers, spark my creativity, as I challenge myself to give a new life to these humble materials that have served their original purpose. For me, repurposing the ordinary materials we discard, is an expression of resilience.

I like to say "one person's trash is another person's canvas."

Review Excerpts

"Although the artists all share the immigrant experience, few apply themselves to studying their adopted land as thoughtfully as Felipe Galindo of Mexico. His drawings, in ink, watercolor or pastel, are on materials that most people discard as trash. Thus, on a cake box he depicts a delicatessen with beer signs using the plastic insert as a window; a bus transfer is grounds for a vignette of a couple waiting at a bus stop, and so on. For an adult, changing countries is like learning to walk again. Mr. Galindo's scratchy little observations sum up the awkwardness of it all."

From "The Immigrant Experience in the 90's" review of the exhibition "Beyond The Borders" at the Bronx Museum, by Vivien Raynor, *The New York Times*, 3/6/1994.

18 WC THE NEW YORK TIMES, SUNDAY, MARCH 6, 1994

ART

The Immigrant Experience in the 90's

By VIVIEN RAYNOR

THE BRONX

WITH "Beyond the Borders," the Bronx Museum of the Arts must hope to eat its diversity ake and have it too. Why else would ie guest curator, Betti-Sue Hertz, go all the trouble of locating 30 immigrant artists from 27 countries only to ount a show that in the end celebrates individualism?

Still, with the ebb and flow of peoles now a worldwide manifestation - and one that has done little to romote international understanding - the production deserves attention.

Except for boat people, the ... ow arrive by plane relatively unhuddled and, in the case of the artists mong them, ready to make dislocaon their subject matter — even to apitalize on it. And, unlike their forears, they come with media-fostered lusions, although these are often no ore than updated versions of streets paved with gold." All of hich may explain why "Beyond the oundaries" is arranged under curiusly unhelpful headings like Grounded Transmissions" and "Inrmed Interference."

In any case, the viewer, as usual, is ft holding the bag, determining hich of its esthetic contents were nported and which acquired in the nited States, particularly by the arts who have studied here.

Among the show's redeeming feares are the biographical stateents, some of them quite poignant or example, Dinh Le, from Vietnam, peaks of having followed the Confuian doctrines of obedience to elders nd loyalty to family until overhelmed by the American " 'me' vale system." The result in the show is series of large C-prints featuring olls with the faces of Cher, Michael ackson, Vanilla Ice and others.

After these idols, all depicted withut clothes, come the fantasies of milya Dunayets. Most are dark penil and watercolor landscapes inhabitd by pale-faced humans and polyorphs reminiscent of Chagall. Ms unayets comes from Ukraine and, eling "like an alien in a cruel and stless world," she admits to using rt as a form of self-defense.

Anold Étienne explains that he is a elf-taught painter because there ere no art schools in his part of aiti. But his high-keyed landscapes, ough brimming with incidents, like bus falling off a hill, are too well rganized to be regarded as wholly naive. Formerly an engineer, Moses Daramola from Nigeria is now an artist working with sand and colored beads on mahogany panels to produce intricate patterns, like that of a tall woman bent double over a red pot.

From this to Mo Bahc's "Traditional Breeze II" is a few feet and many psychological miles. As if there were no alternative, Mr. Bahc devotes himself to reconciling the irreconcilable, notably his own country, South Korea, with the United States. He does it with paint, video or, as here, with a treelike assemblage involving hand-held fans and the electric kind.

Among the many artists taking a political route is Shirin Neshat, an Iranian molded by five years' study at the University of California at Berkeley. On a recent visit to her native land, Ms. Neshat was impressed to see women wearing the veil again but at the same time doing military service. In the photographer's larger-than-lifesize black and white prints, they pose with rifles.

Pacita Abad draws inspiration from the art of Melanesia. She produces large, bright wall hangings of ferocious figures made with cowrie shells, beads, a mirror and other objects.

Although the artists all share t immigrant experience, few app themselves to studying their adopt land as thoughtfully as Felipe Galin of Mexico. His drawings, in ink, w tercolor or pastel, are on materi that most people discard as tra Thus, on a cake box he depicts delicatessen with beer signs, us the plastic insert as a window; a b transfer is grounds for a vignette o couple waiting at a bus stop, and on. For an adult, changing countries like learning to walk again. Mr. Gali do's scratchy little observations su up the awkwardness of it all.

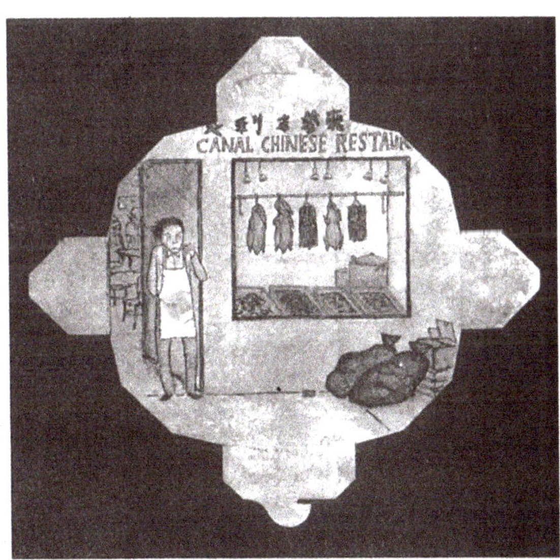

"Roasted Ducks," watercolor, pastel and ink on Chinese food container by Felipe Galind

"A different kind of levelling occurs when one encounters the fresh paradigm of an unfamiliar culture: everything is novel, even strange, since nothing comes to one conditioned by memory or old ways of looking. It is with this attitude of surprise that Felipe Galindo, a native of Cuernavaca, Mexico, who now lives in New York, infuses new life into the slight practice of street caricature. Ephemera, such as a napkin from Nathan's Famous Deli, a shopping bag from Saks Fifth Avenue, or the odd-shaped food container from the Chinese take-out, are collected as souvenirs and converted into either a drawing surface or a collage material. Typically, Galindo superimposes and synthesizes his drawn vignette with the existing graphics of the found surface. Thus, in a scene of a coffee shop, one finds -printed on a flattened coffee cup that doubles as a counter for the drawn characters- vulgarized depictions of the acropolis and Zeus. The icons of Greek culture now serve as design motifs framing the phrase: "WE ARE PLEASED TO SERVE YOU." Although akin to the tourist's snapshot, Galindo images are made intimate through the intercession of the artist's hand, since to draw from life is to domesticate, and is the means by which the artist can map out his new surroundings."

Linh Dihn, critic-in-residence,
Animated exhibition, Art in General, June 1994

"To a show that sometimes groans under its own seriousness, Felipe Galindo's disarming street-scene caricatures lend a welcome leavening touch. A native of Cuernavaca, Mexico, Galindo rings his immigrant eye to New York's City richly variegated landscape, drawing and painting amusing vignettes on such paper castoffs as a bag from Nathan's Famous, a subway map and a flattened Chinese take-out container, incorporating their logos and graphics into his work. His Coney Island beach scene, for example, is on Nathan's bag, with its printed image of the giant roller coaster in the background. To this viewer's taste, the best piece is his drawing of a Chinese restaurateur having a smoke on his doorway. The food container that is Galindo's drawing surface has been splayed, so its decoratively scalloped shape seems like an oriental motif."

From the *Raices Hispanas/Hispanic Roots* exhibition, Mills Pond House, Long Island. Review by Karin Lipson in *Newsday*, 9/22/1995.

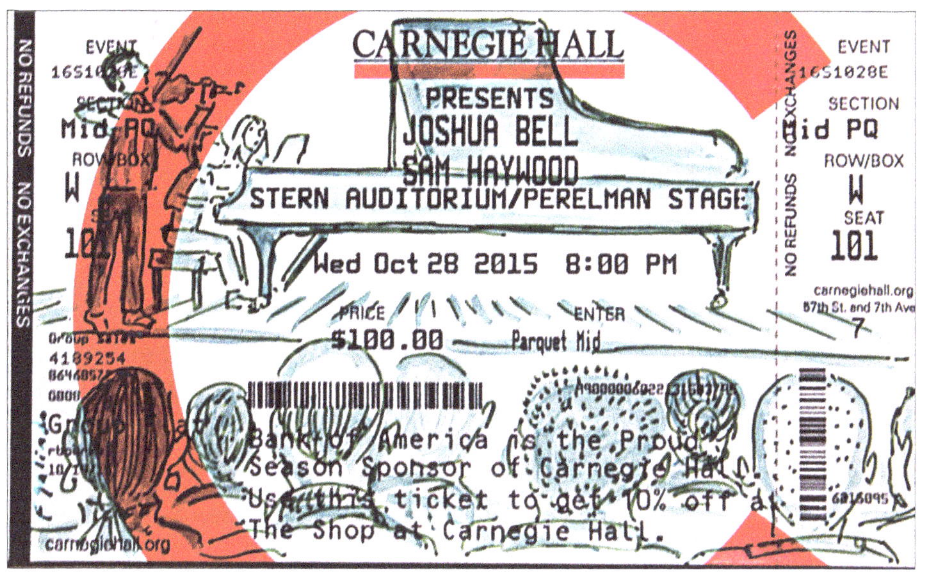

"In a new show entitled "New York Stories", Galindo, who signs his *New Yorker* cartoons as Feggo, has drawn people on found objects ever since he moved to the city from Mexico. The show is as witty as his cartoons. Galindo makes clever use of his ability as an artist as well as the materials he selects. In one drawing, Saints in the City, three people sport halos made from the foil of yogurt containers. In another, an old Habitat bag is the canvas for a painting of a homeless man asleep on a park bench... Galindo said the muse can strike at any moment. He has about 100 sketchbooks filled with drawings of people on the subway, restaurants and parks. Museums are also a wealth of inspiration... Matching objects with art takes different paths. At times, he'll re-draw riders on subway or bus maps and add ink and paint. Or he'll transform any found object into a work of art... The plastic lids of coffee containers still haven't given up the mysteries to Galindo. He's intrigued by the lines and openings. "I still don't know what to do with that," he said. "Every time I have coffee, I look and say: What can I do with this?"

From *Stories, Spoken in Strokes* review of exhibition at the Mark Miller Gallery by Sherry Mazzocchi in the *Manhattan Times*, 12/2015.

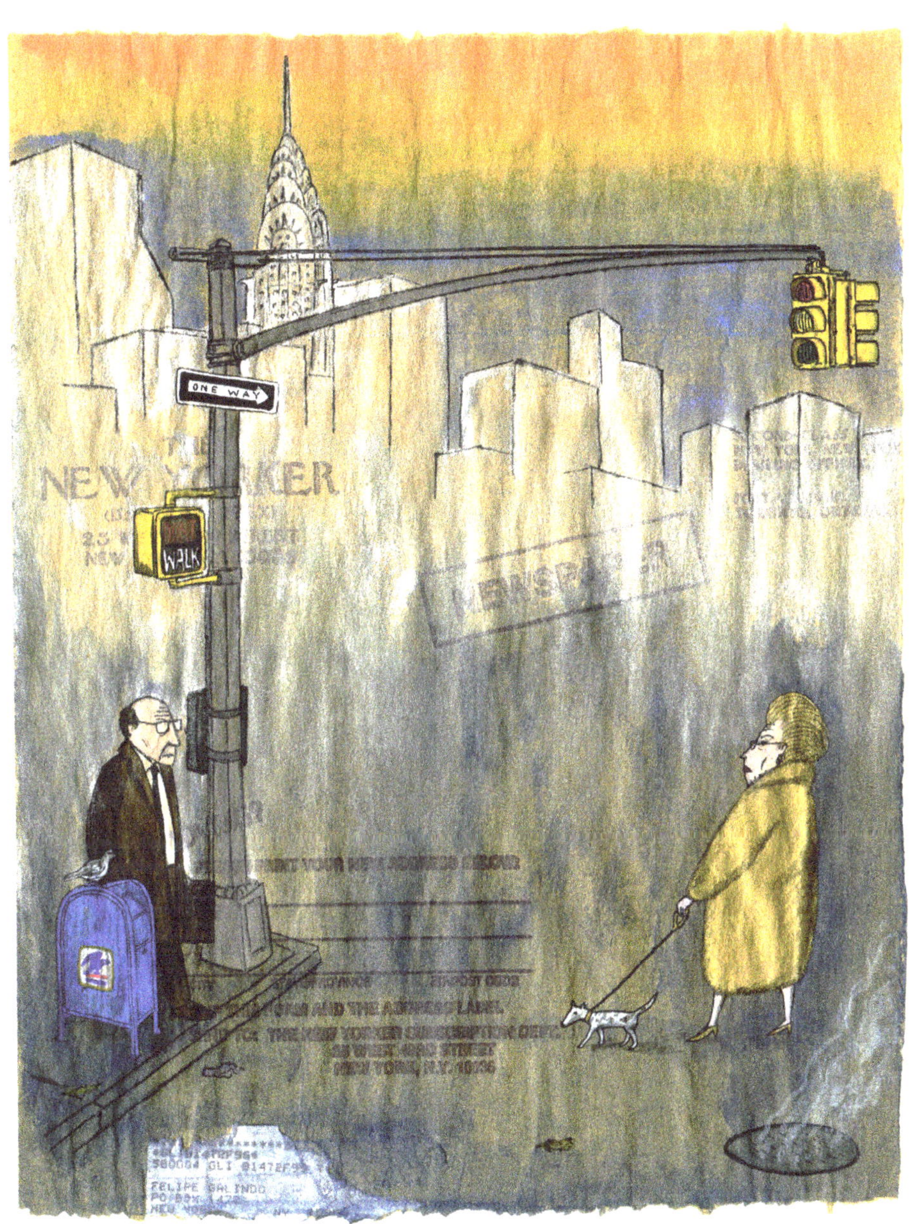
ONE WAY
WALK

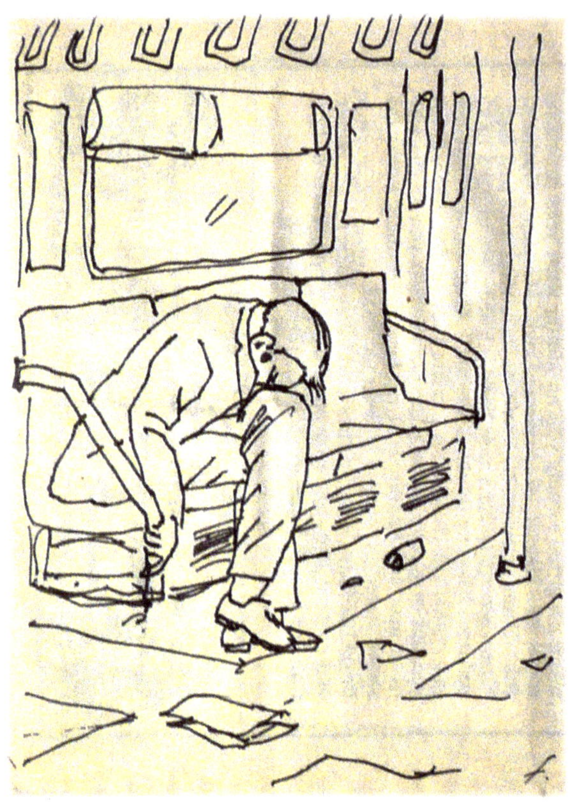

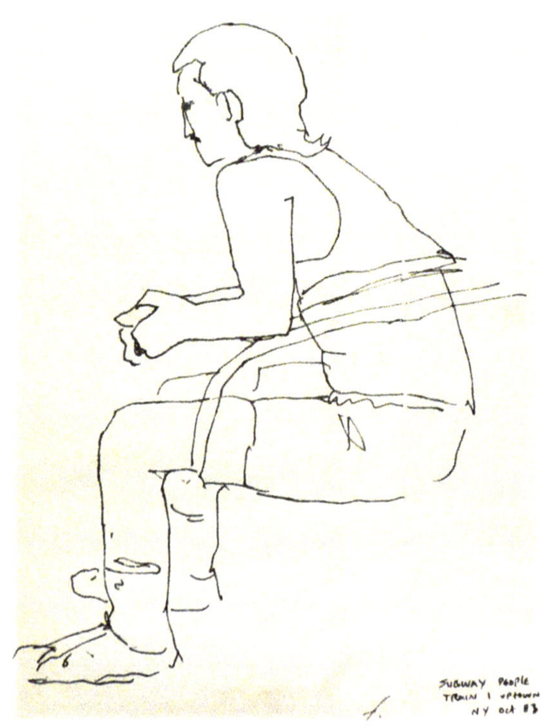
SUBWAY PEOPLE
TRAIN 1 UPTOWN
NY Oct 83

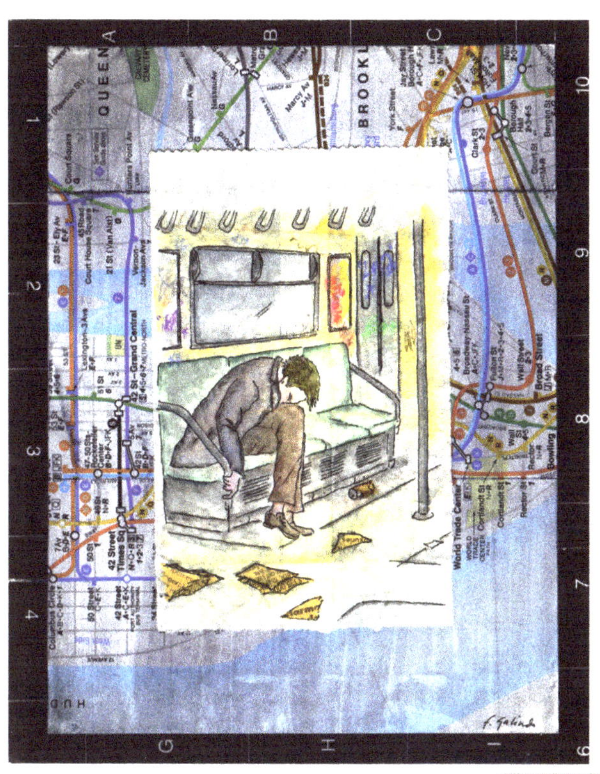

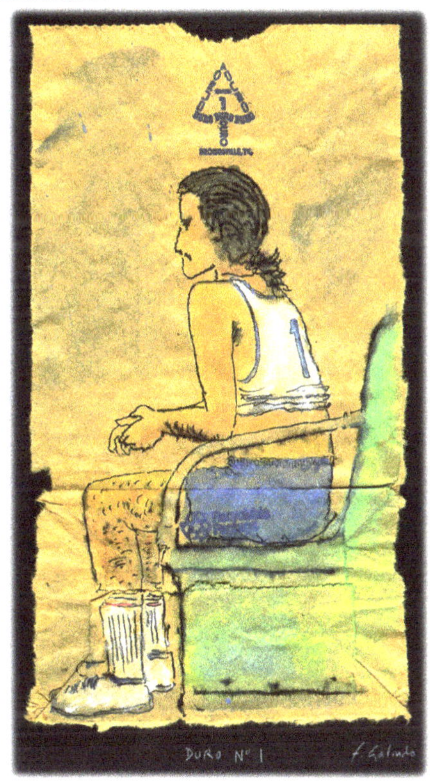
DURO Nº 1
f. Galindo

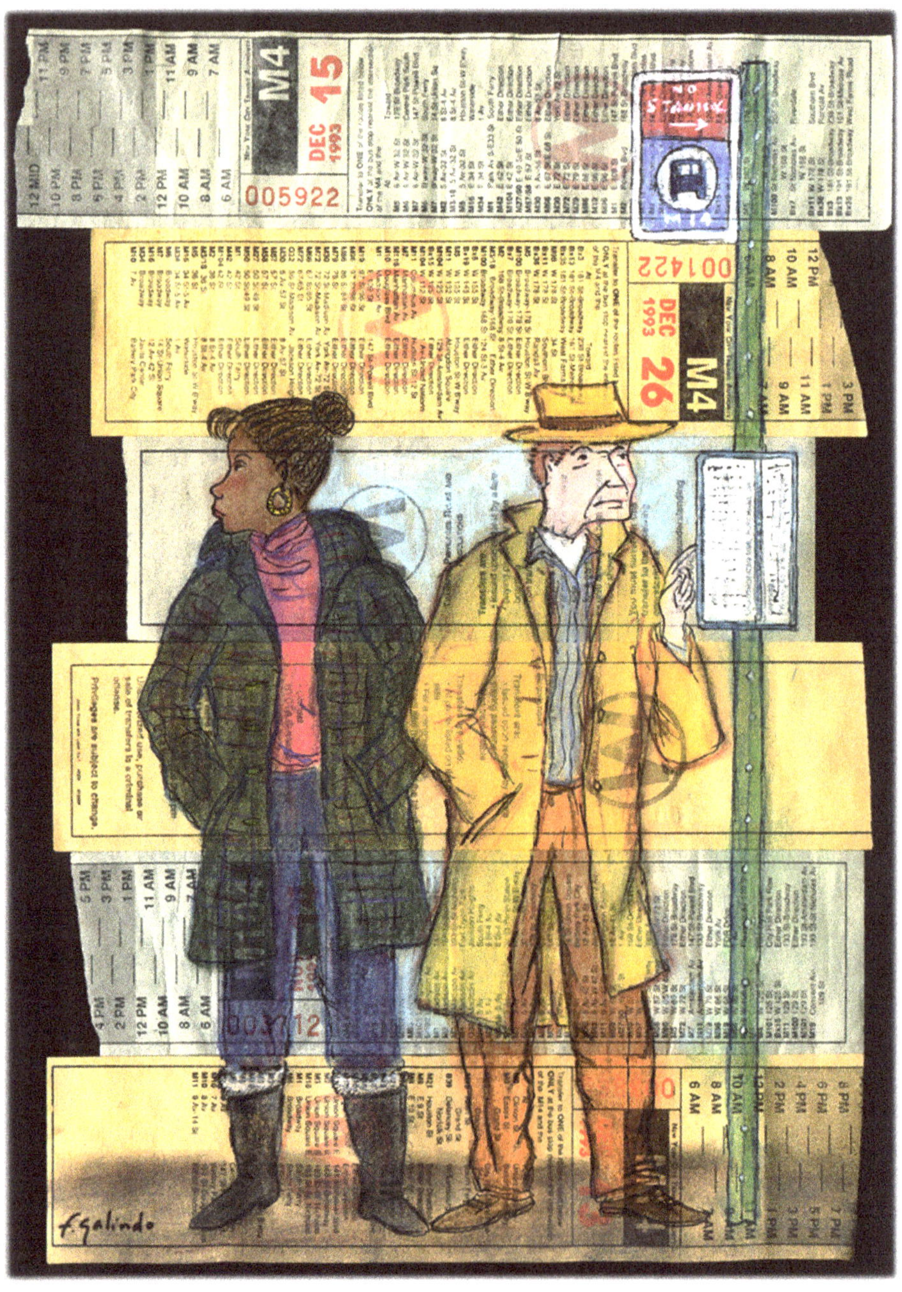
NO STANDING
M14
M4
DEC 15
1993
005922
f. galindo

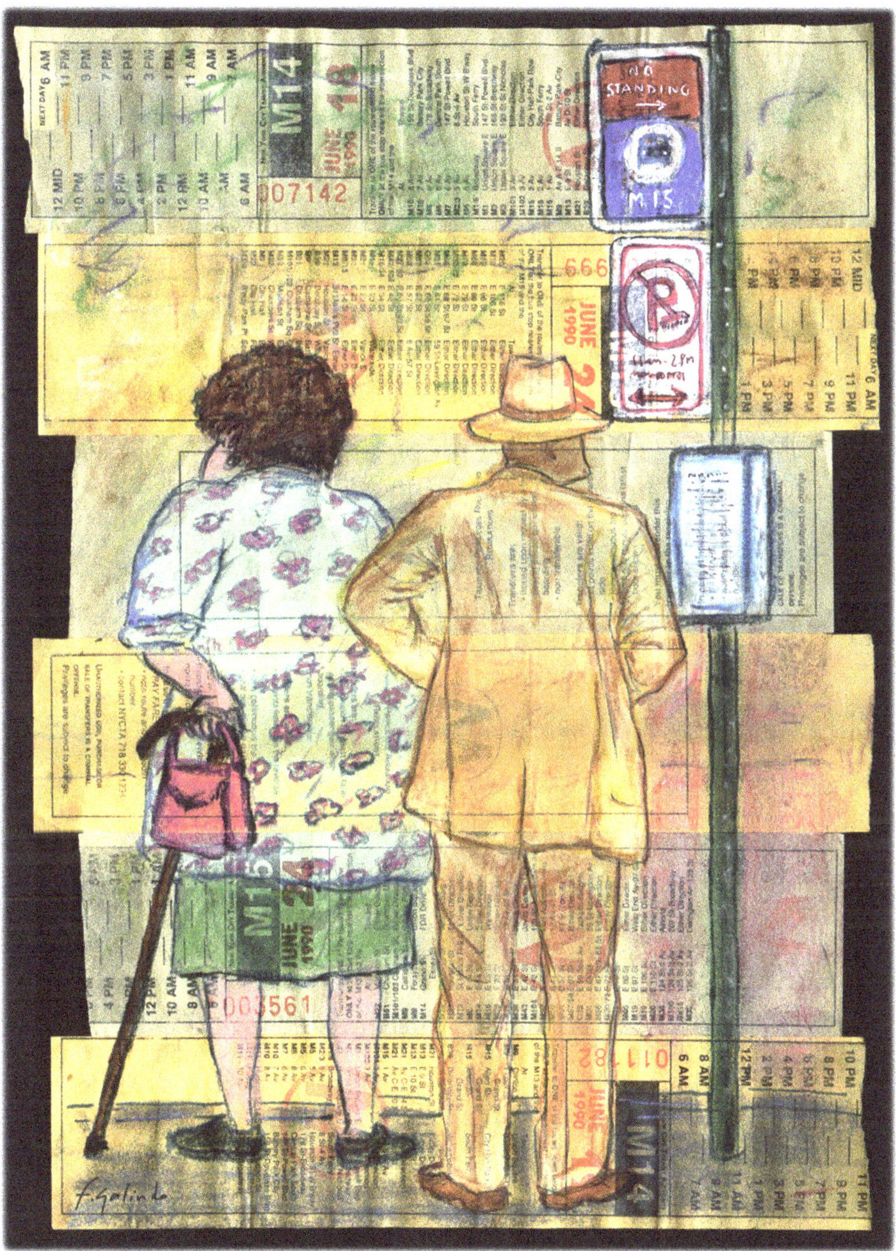
NO STANDING
M15
F. Galindo

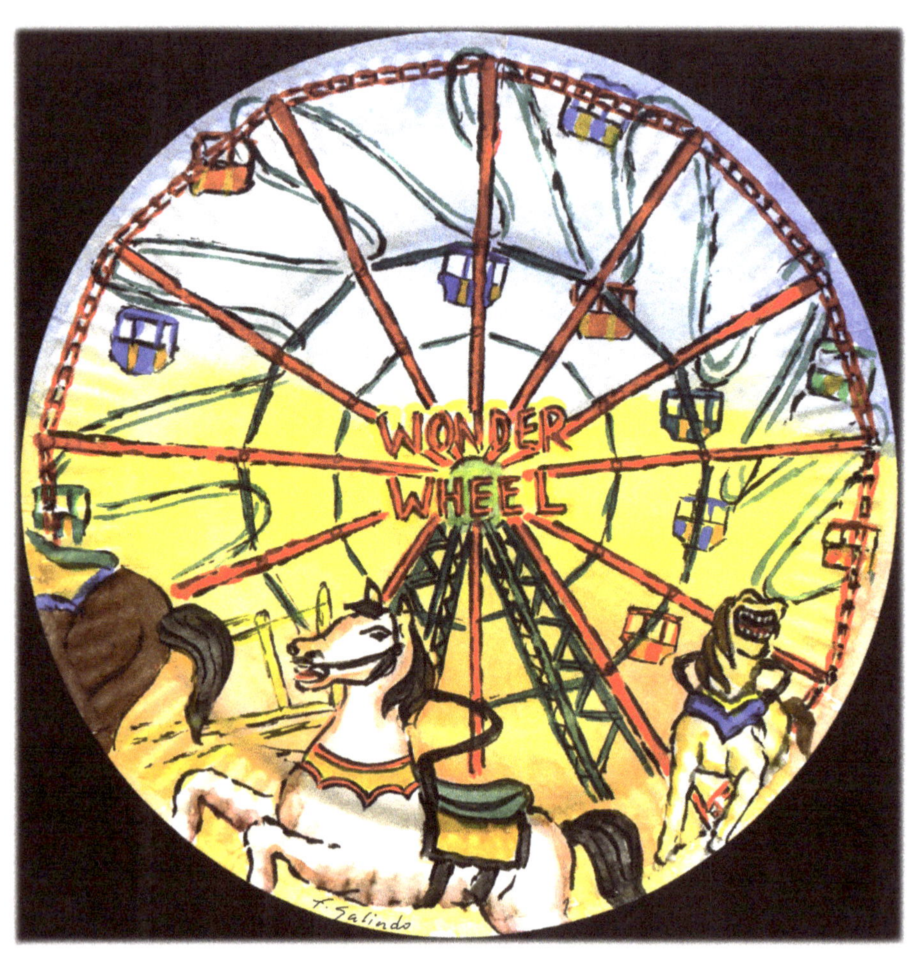
WONDER
WHEEL

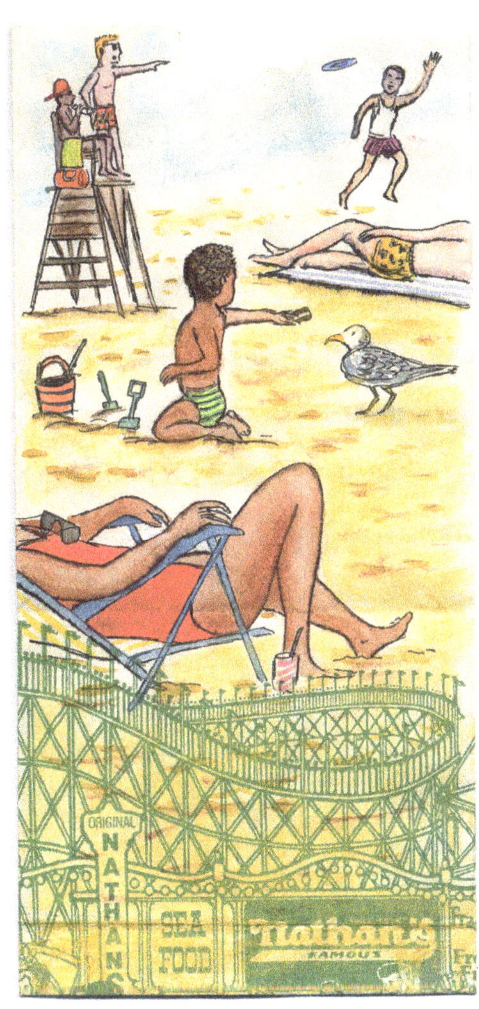
ORIGINAL
NATHANS
SEA FOOD
Nathan's
FAMOUS

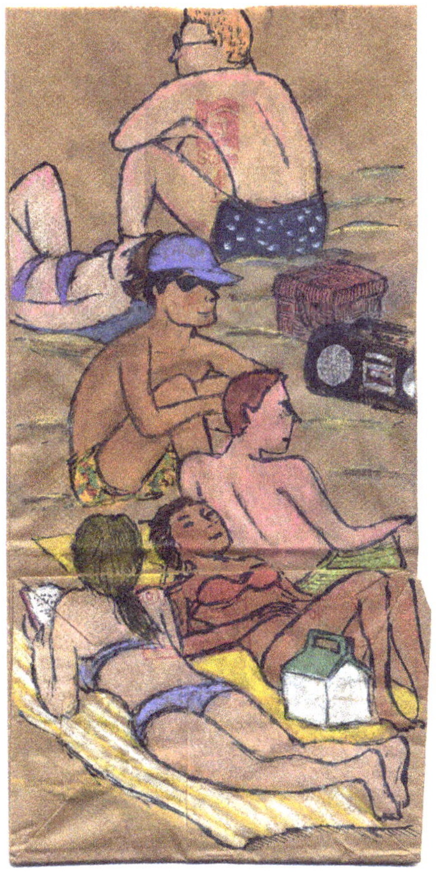

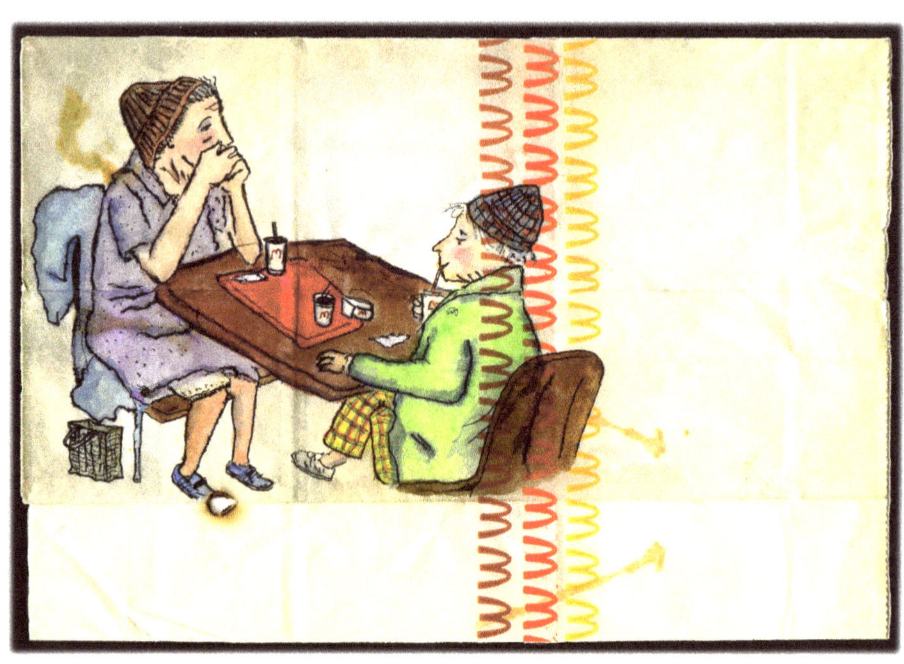

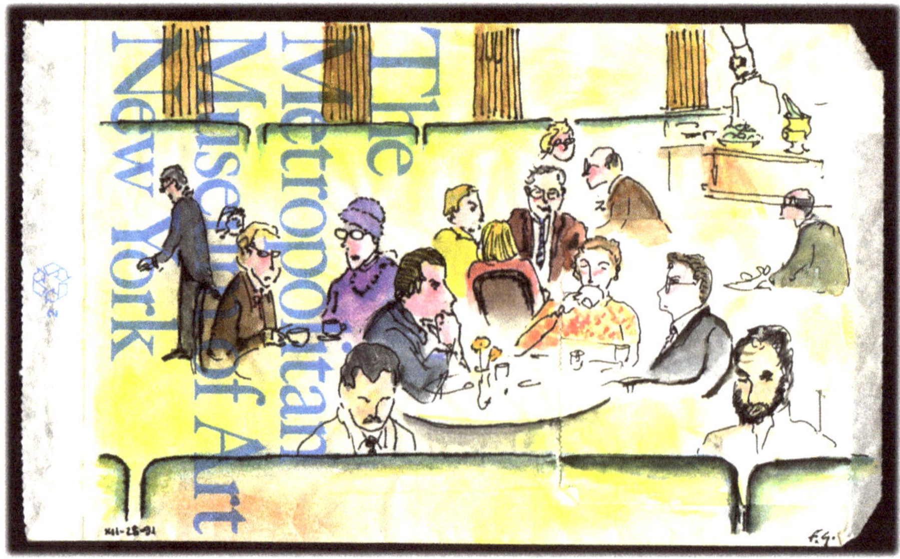
The
Metropolitan
Museum of Art
New York

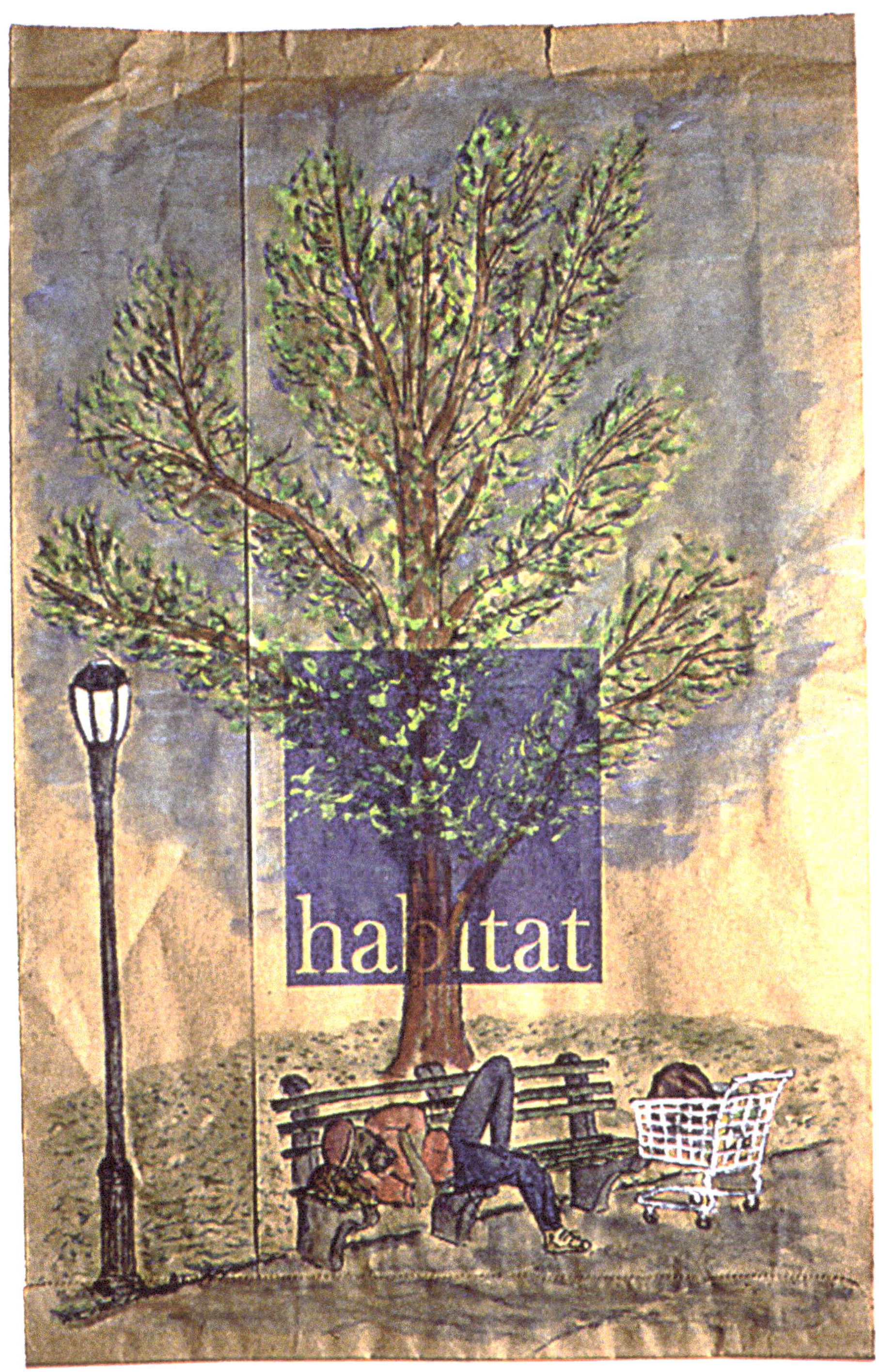
habitat

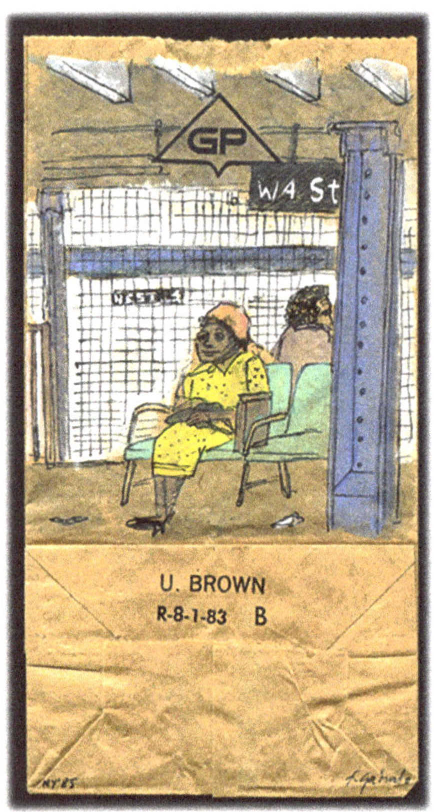
GP
W4 St
U. BROWN
R-8-1-83 B

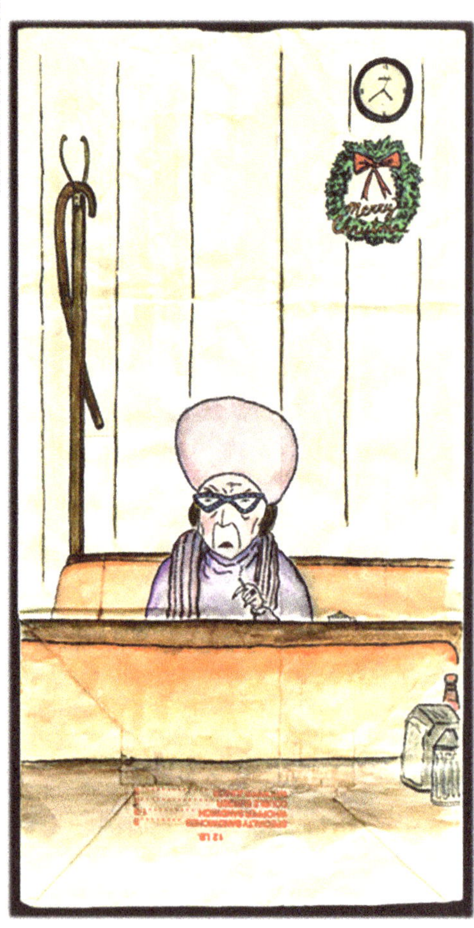
Merry

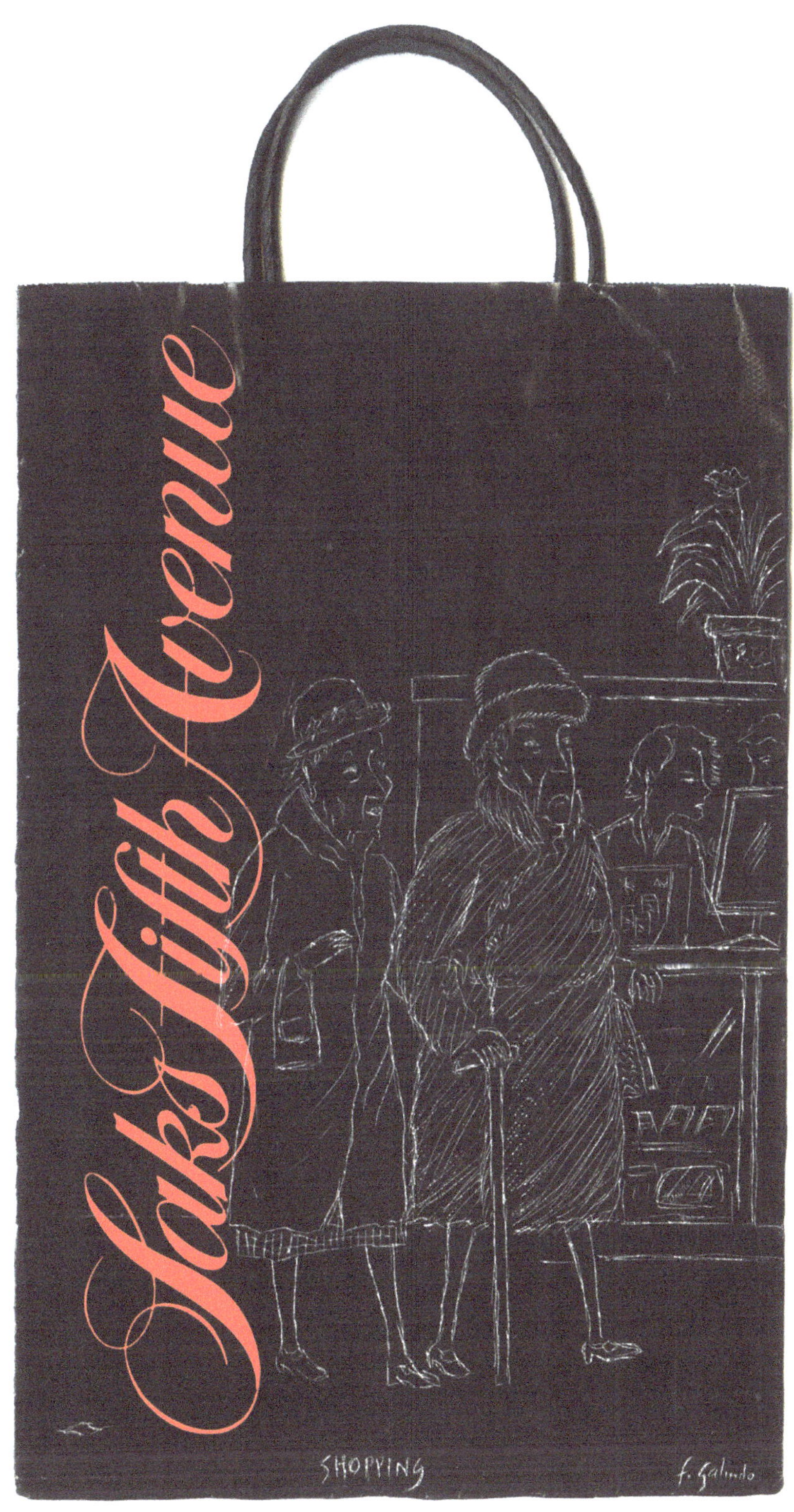
Saks Fifth Avenue
SHOPPING
f. Galindo

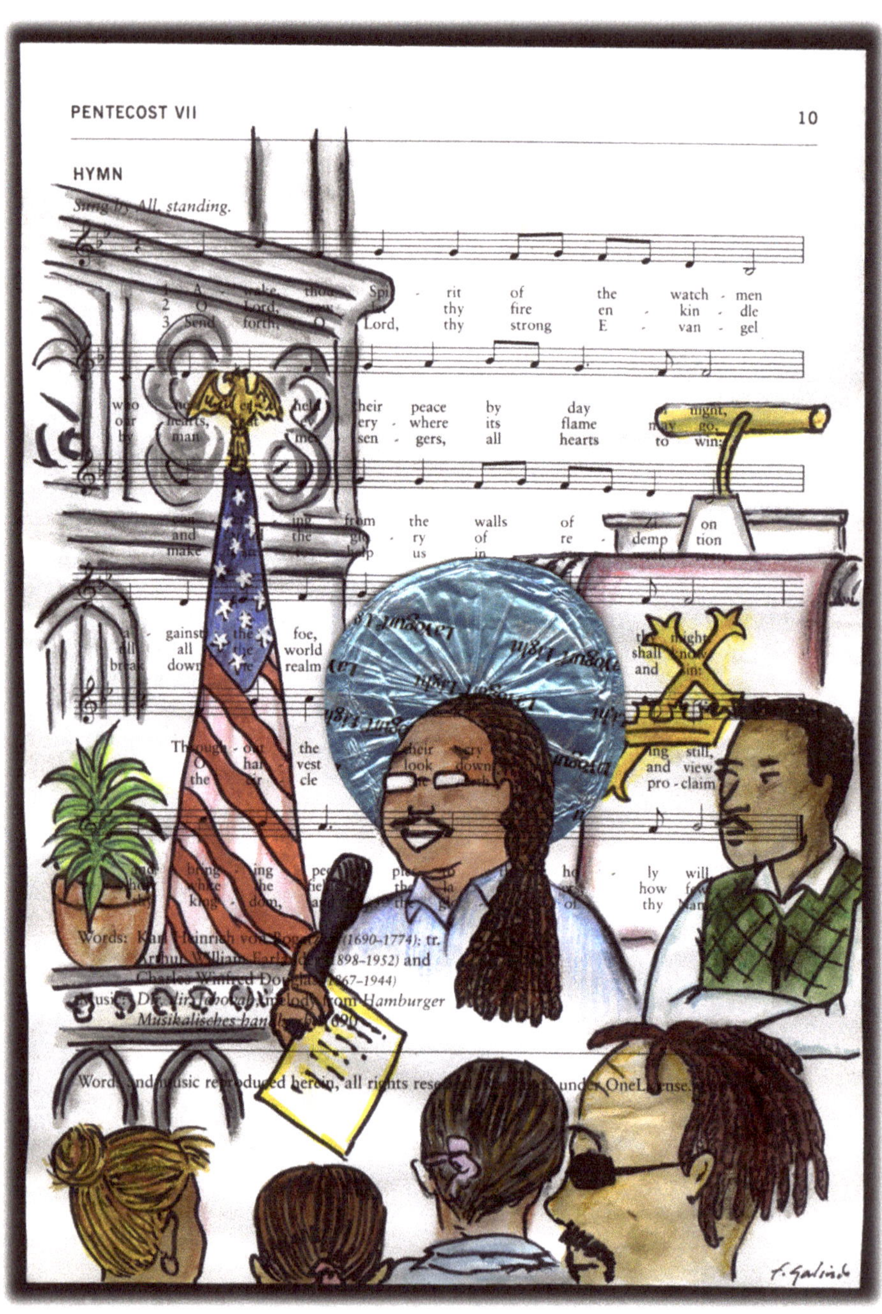
PENTECOST VII
10
HYMN
Sung by All, standing.
1 A - wake, thou Spi - rit of the watch - men
2 O Lord, now thy fire en - kin - dle
3 Send forth, O Lord, thy strong E - van - gel
their peace by day
ery - where its flame
sen - gers, all hearts to win:
from the walls of
re - demp - tion
gainst the foe,
all the world
down the realm
Through - out the
vest
the cle
and view,
pro - claim
ly will
how
thy
(1690–1774); tr.
898–1952) and
Charles Winfred Douglas (1867–1944)
Hamburger
Musikalisches handbuch, 1690
Words and music reproduced herein, all rights reserved under OneLicense

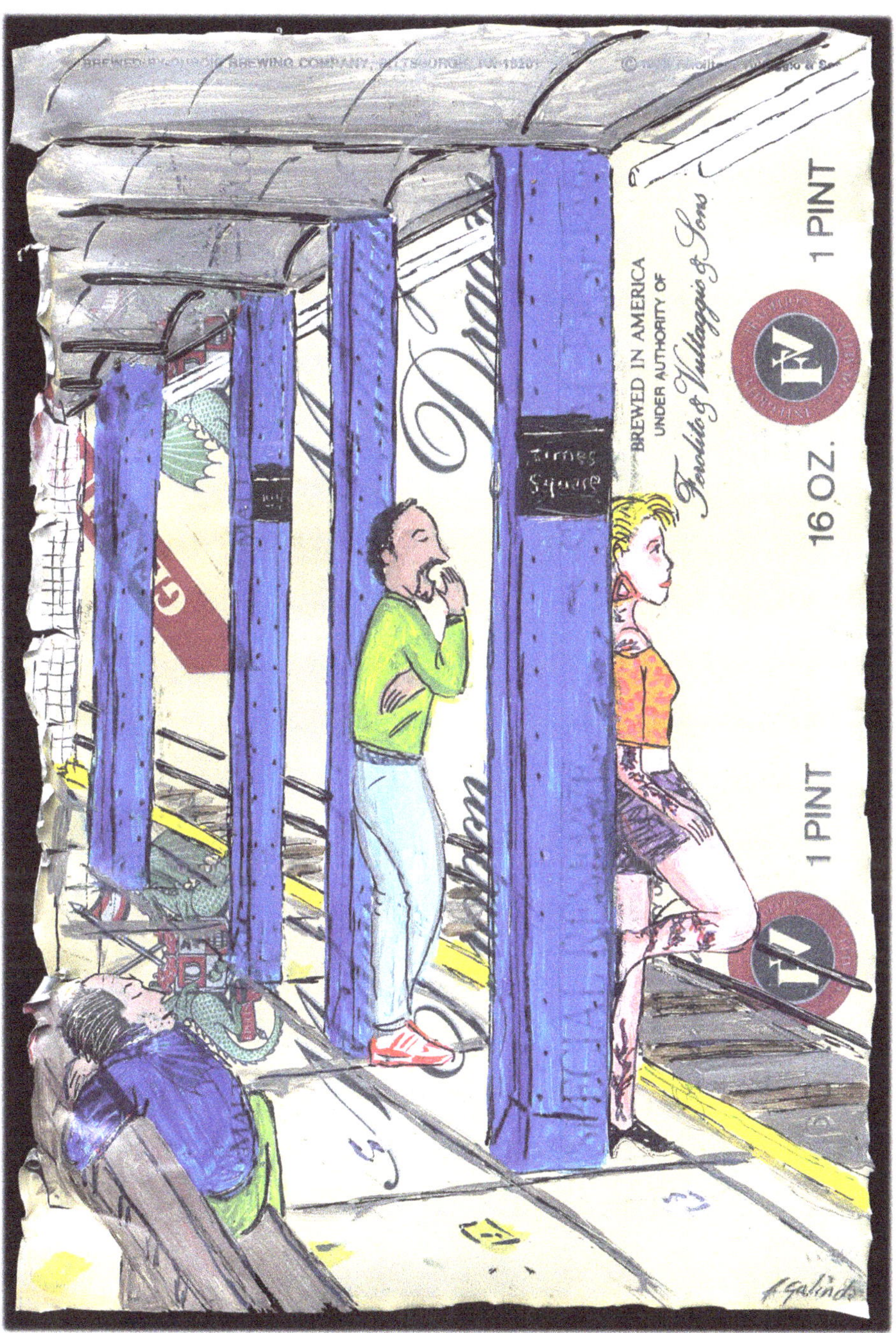
Times Square
BREWED IN AMERICA
UNDER AUTHORITY OF
Ferolito & Vultaggio & Sons
1 PINT
16 OZ.
1 PINT

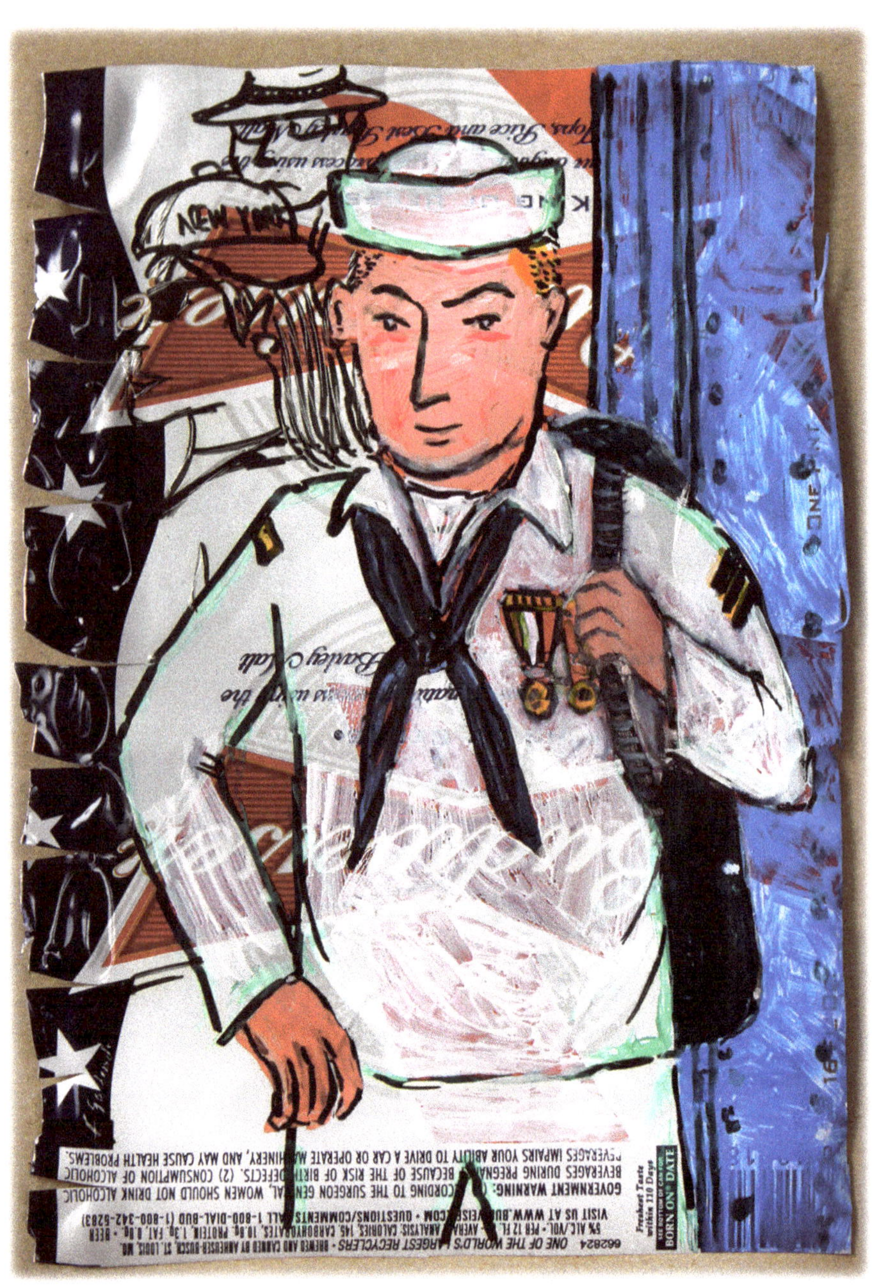
NEW YORK

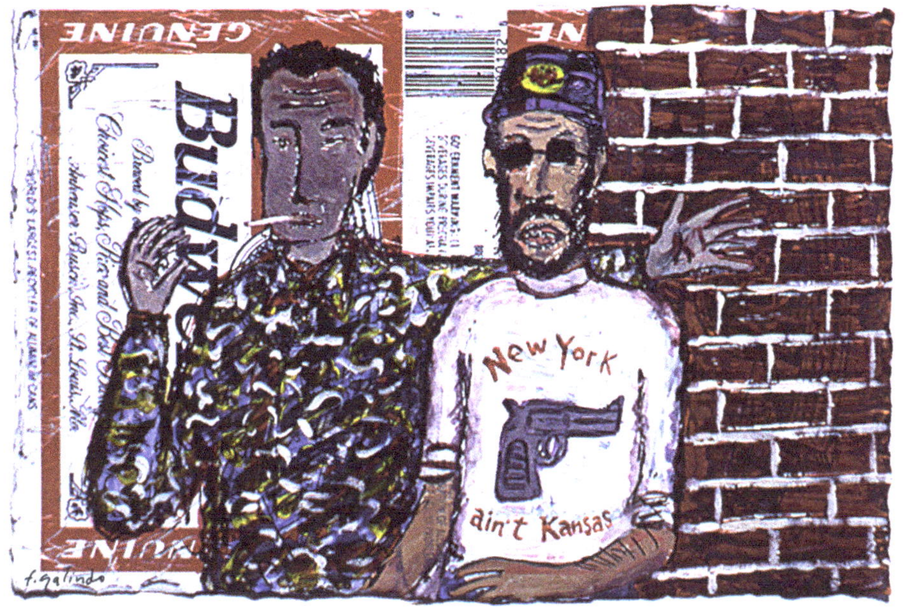

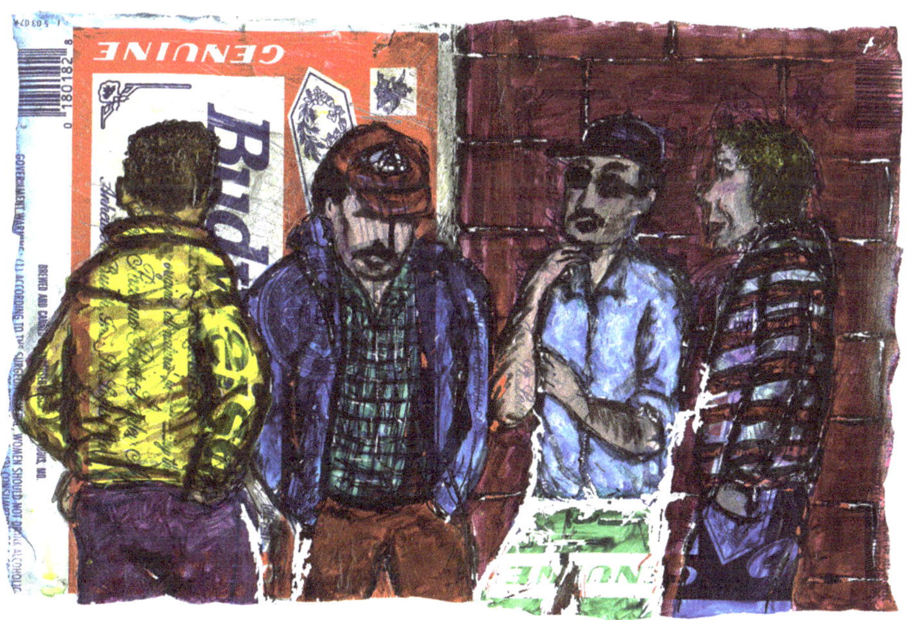

MCMXCVII BUDDIES III f. galindo

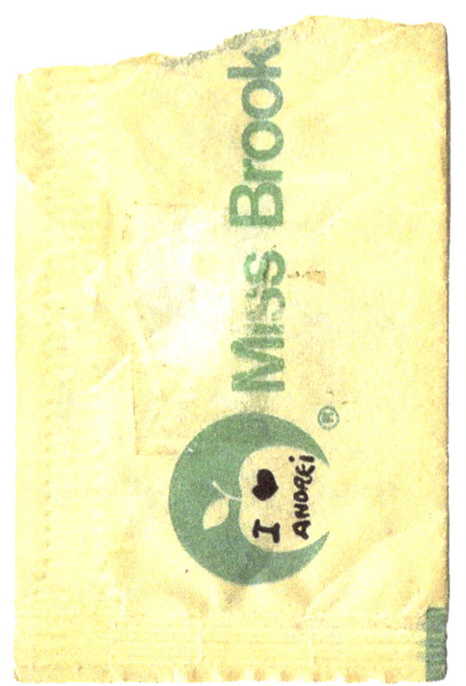
Miss Brook
I ♥ ANDREI

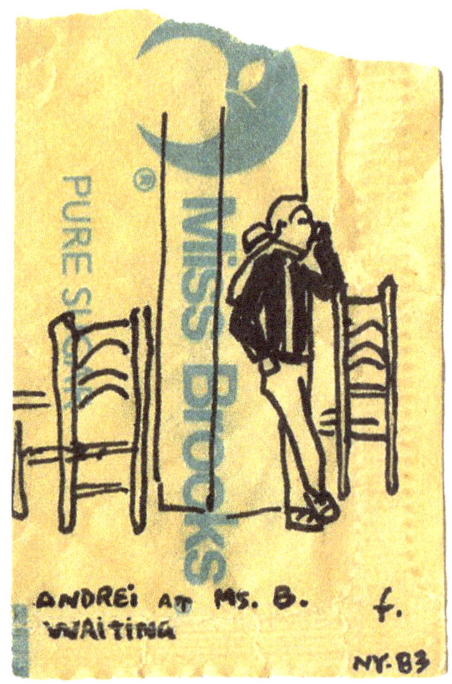
Miss Brooks
ANDREi AT MS. B.
WAITING
f.
NY-83

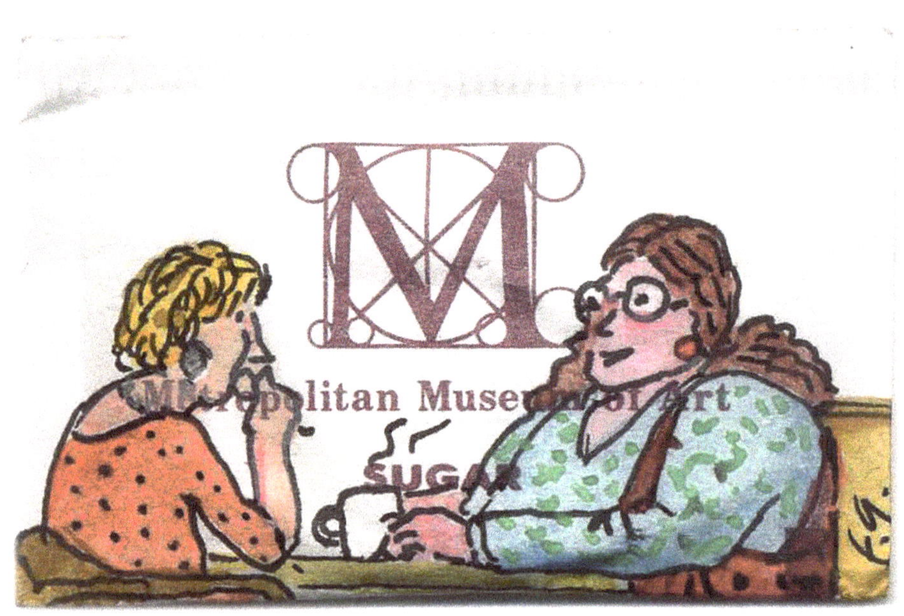

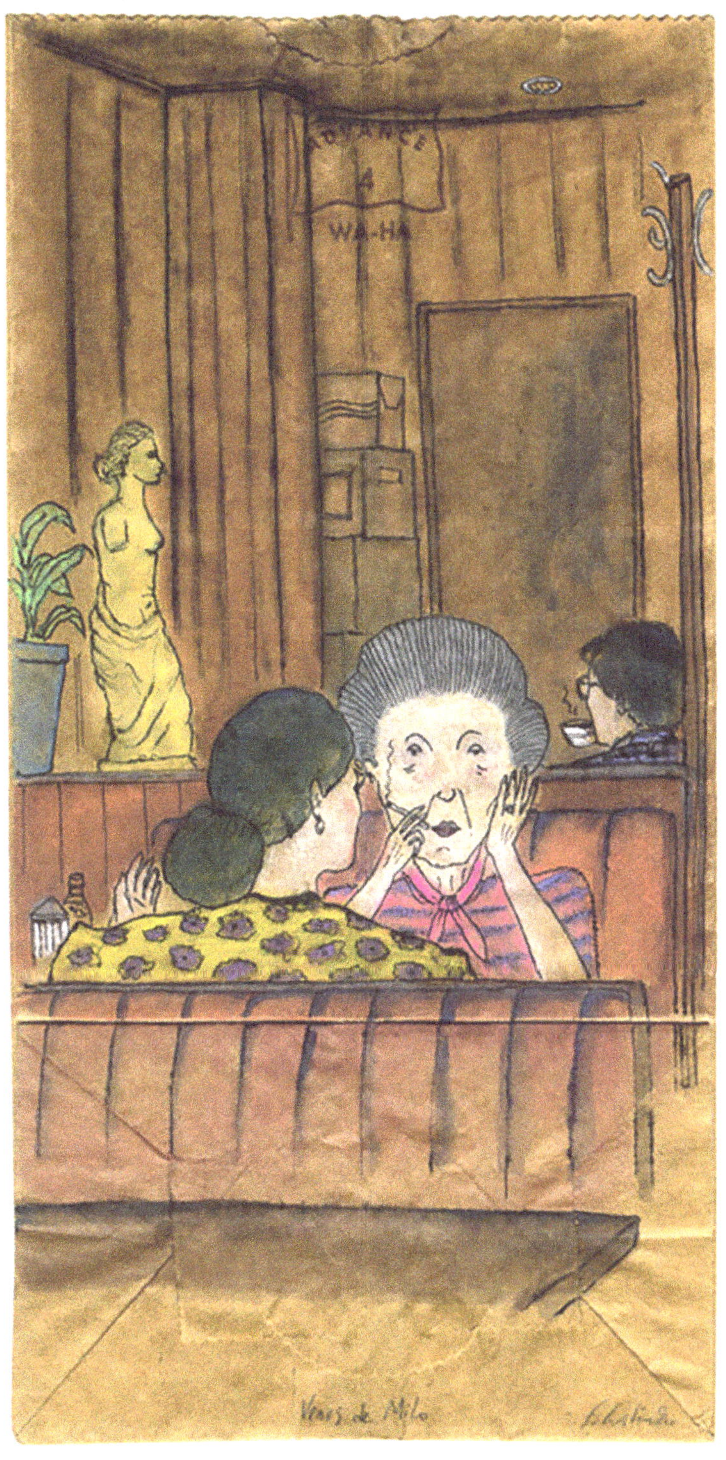
4
WA-HA
Venus de Milo

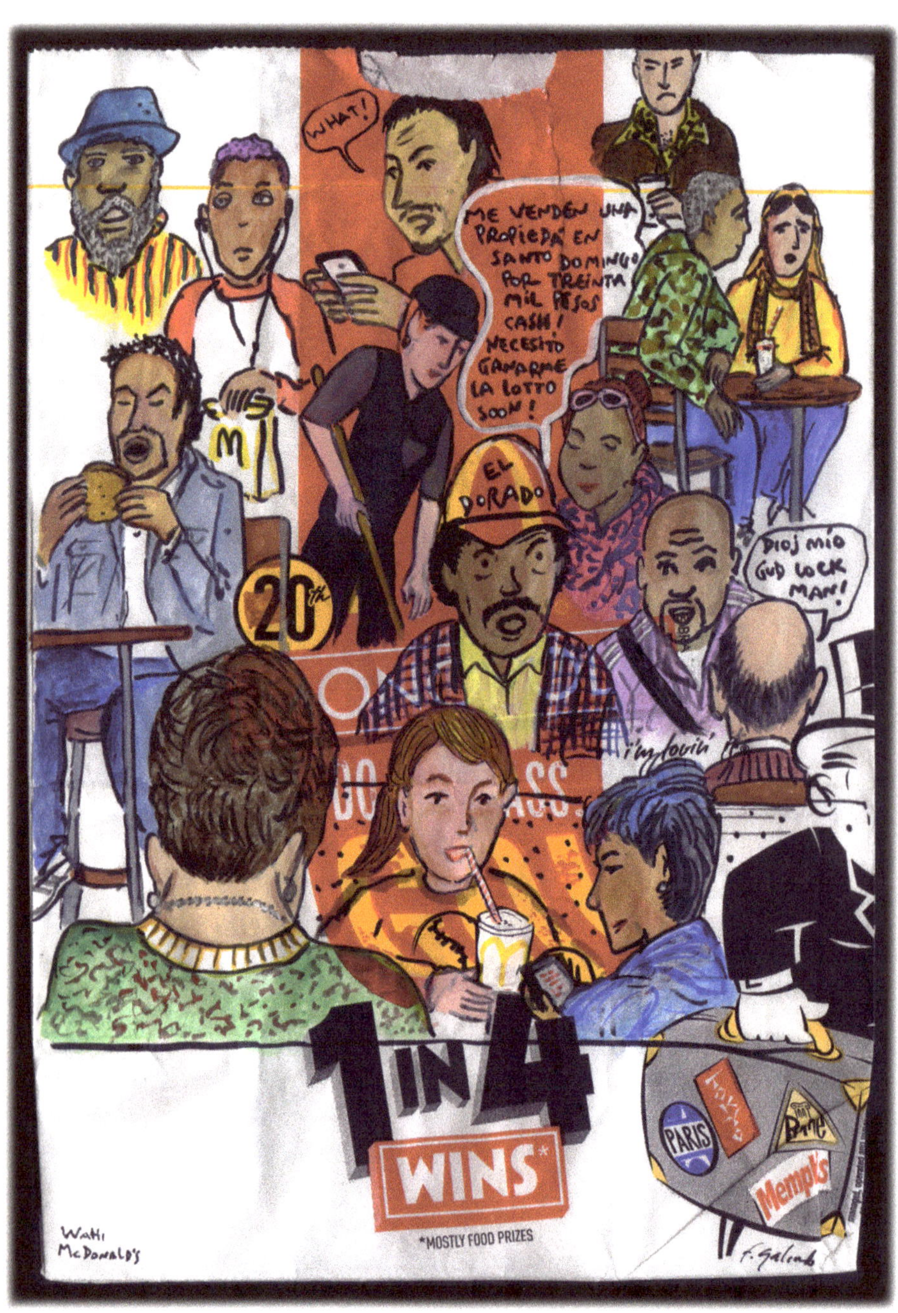
WHAT!
ME VENDEN UNA PROPIEDÁ EN SANTO DOMINGO POR TREINTA MIL PESOS CASH! NECESITO GANARME LA LOTTO SOON!
EL DORADO
Dioj mío Gud lock man!
20th
1 IN 4
WINS*
*MOSTLY FOOD PRIZES
PARIS
Wahi McDonald's
F. Galindo

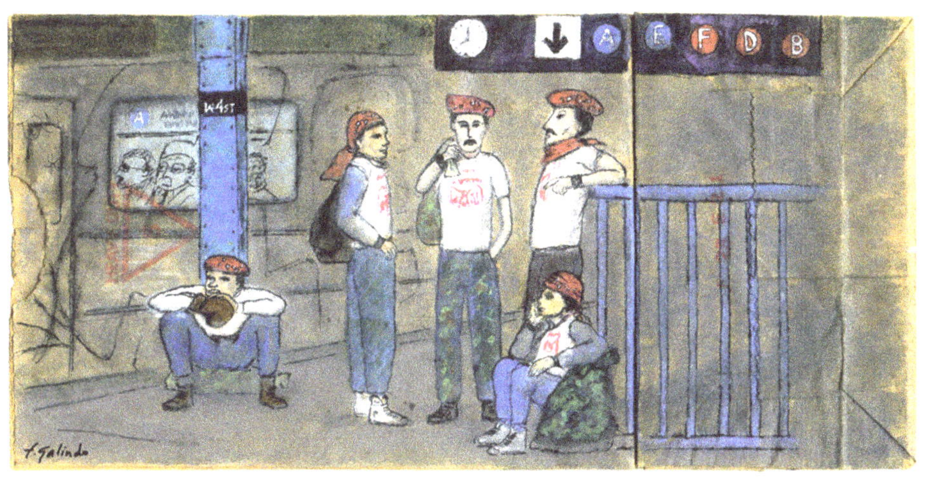
A E F D B
W4ST
F. Galindo

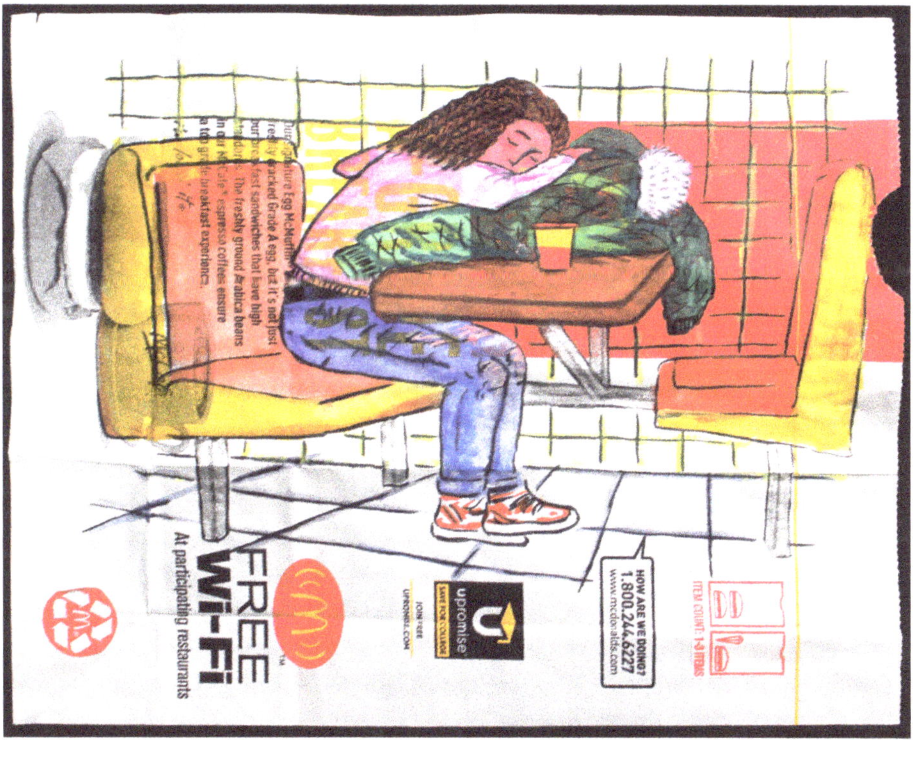

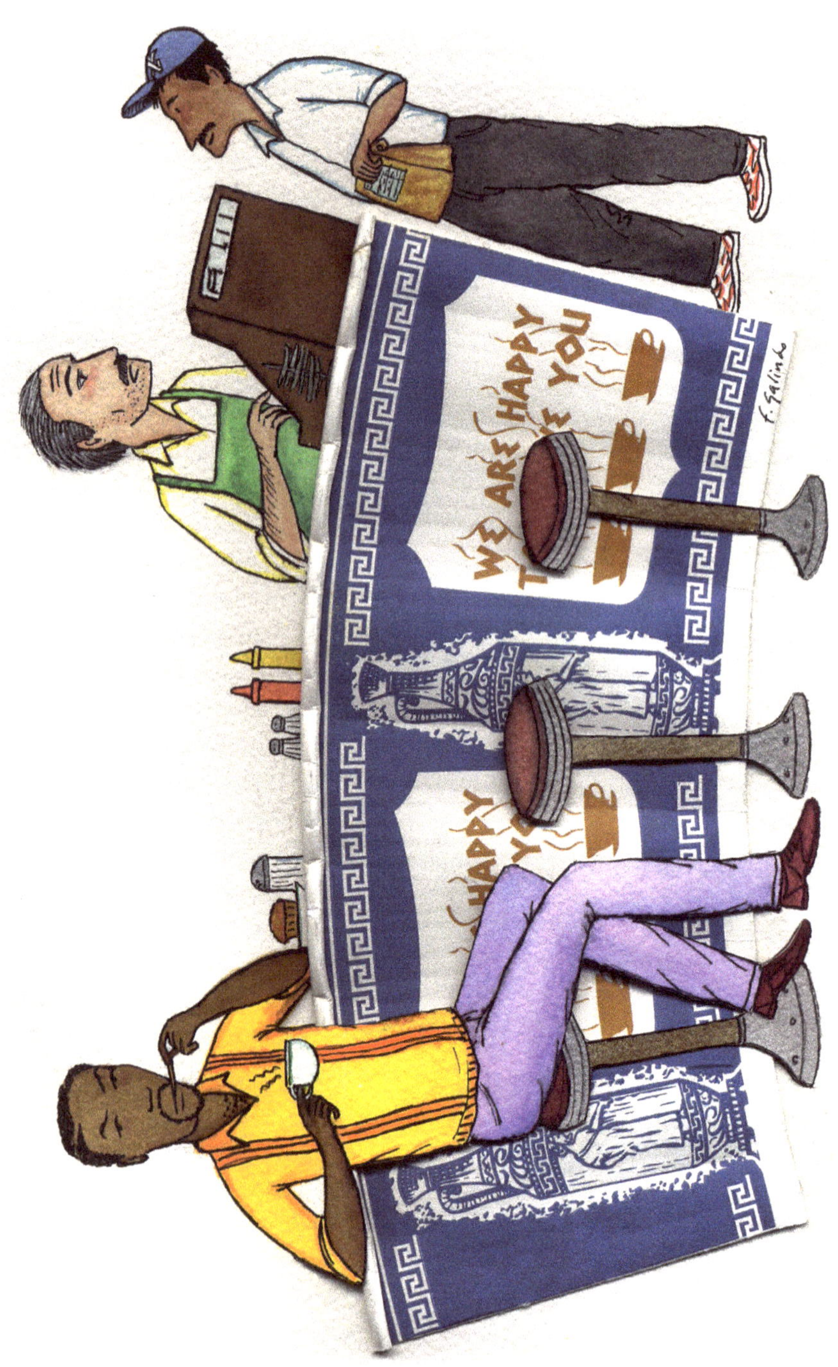
WE ARE HAPPY
HAPPY

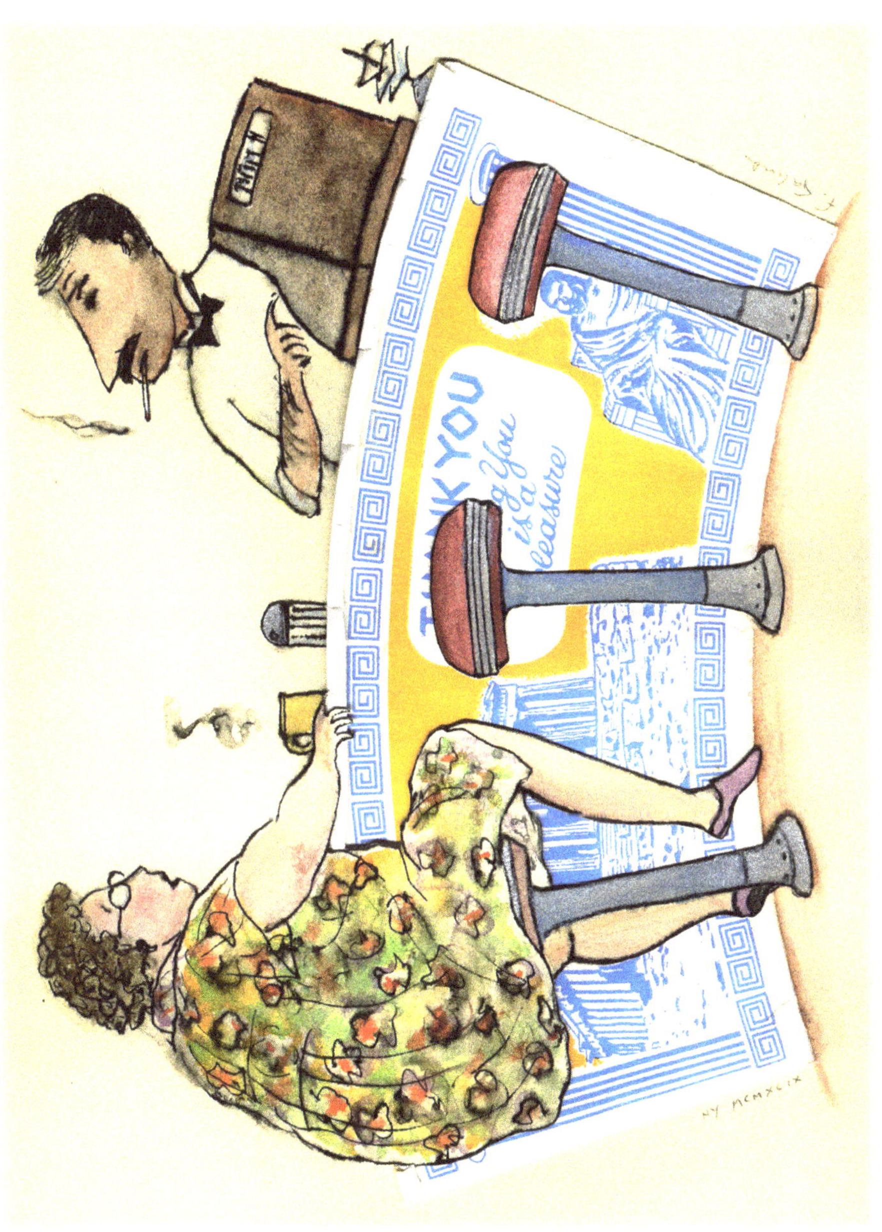
NY MCMXCIX

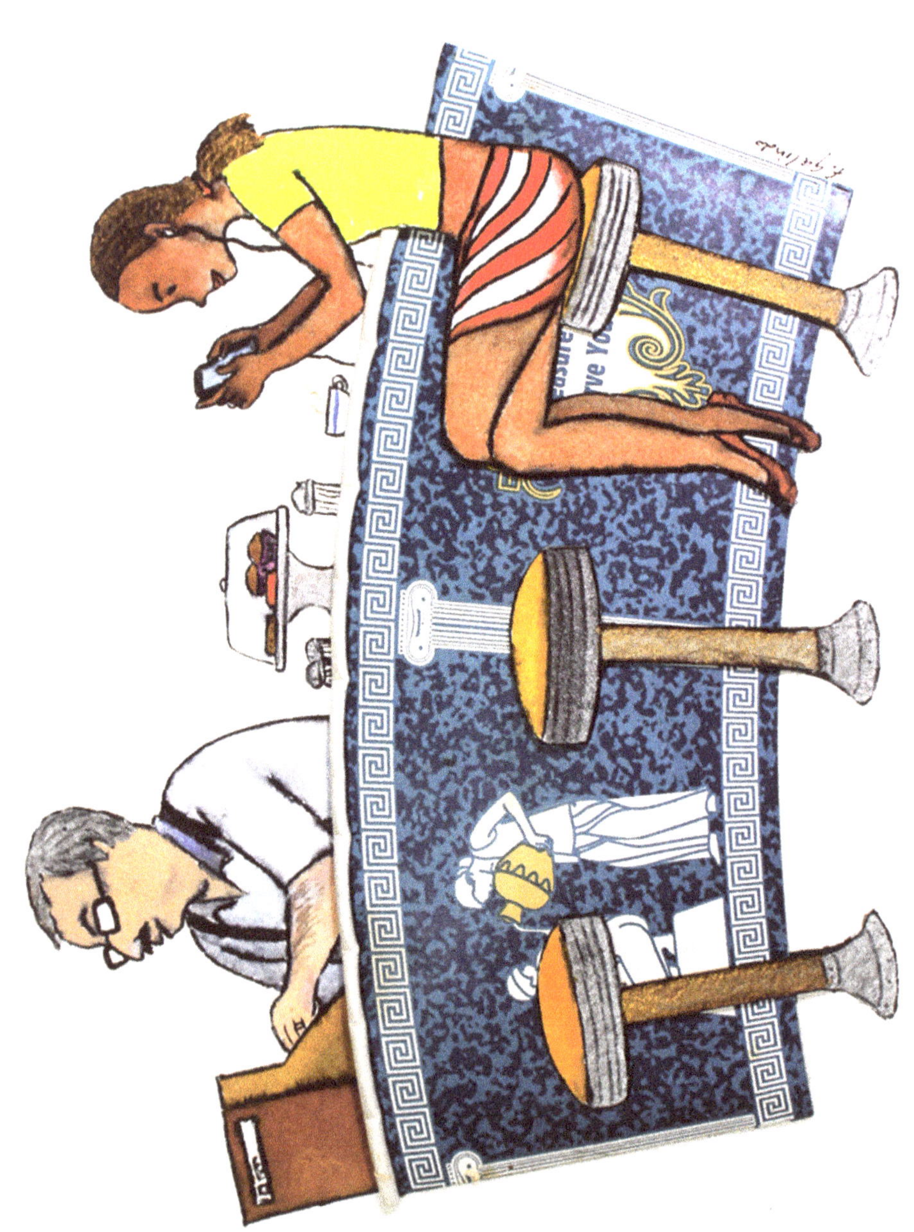

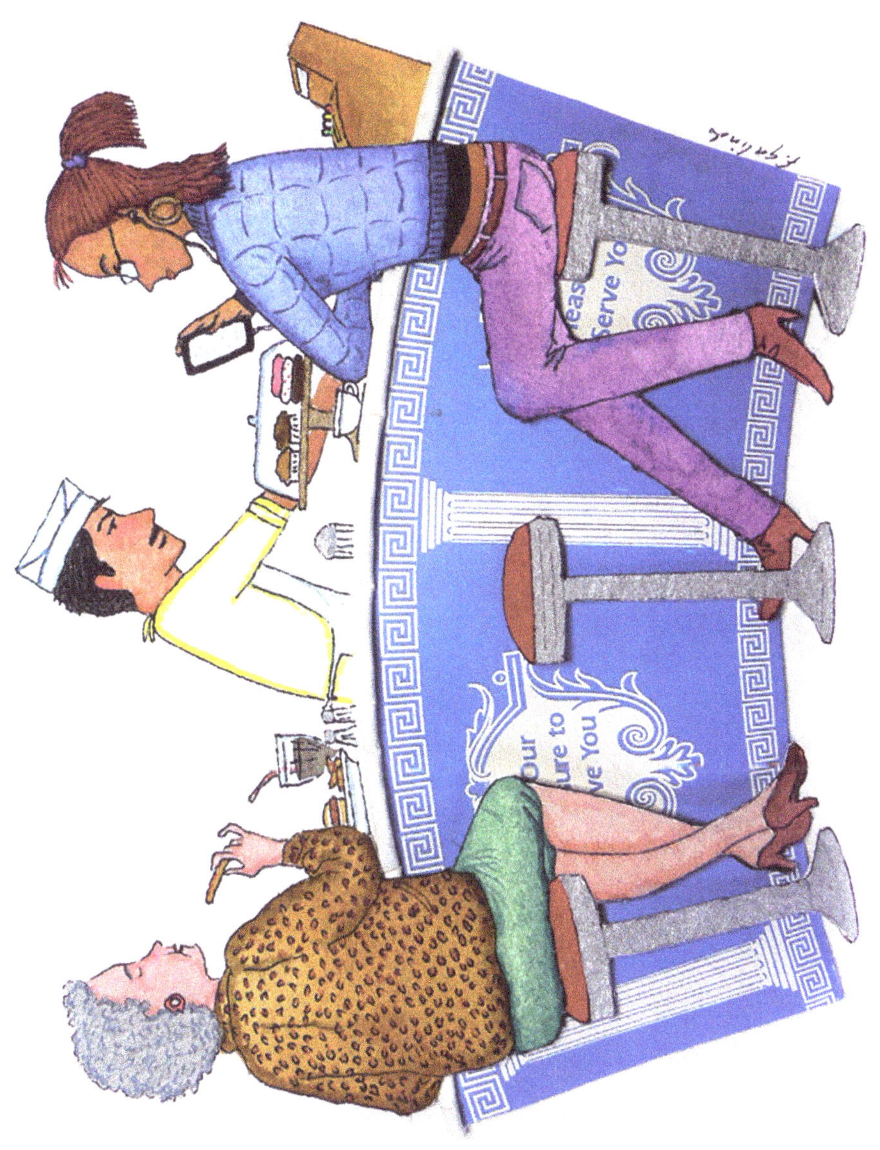

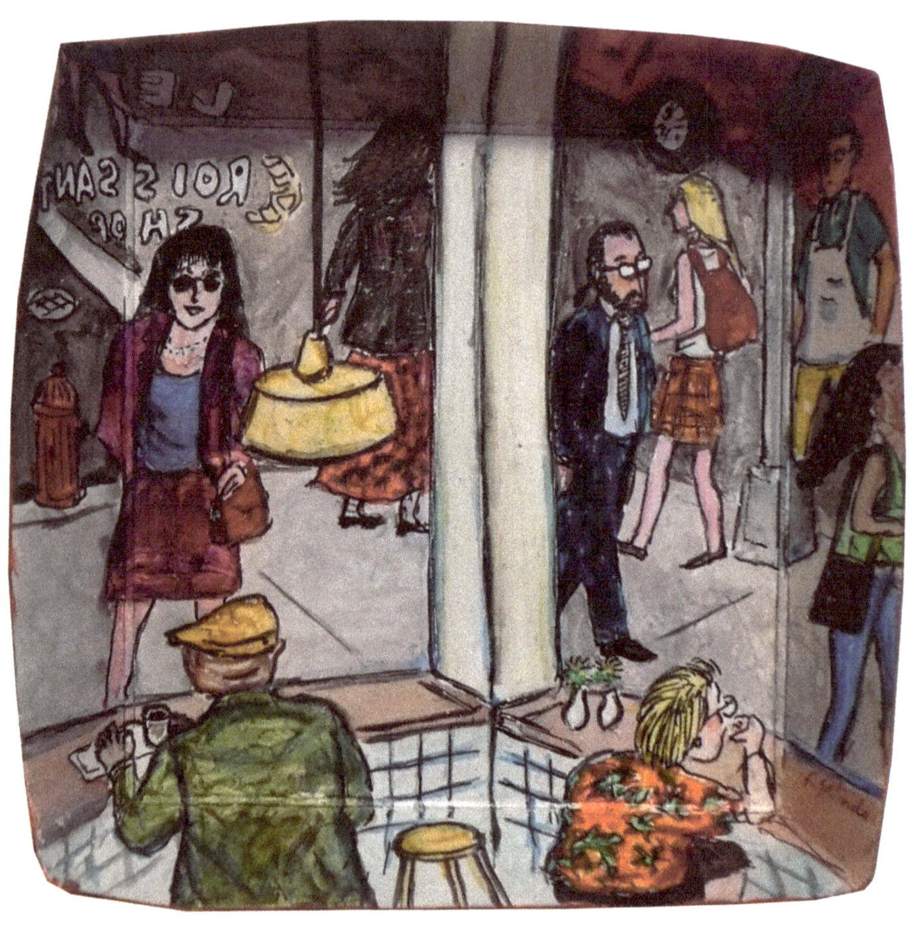

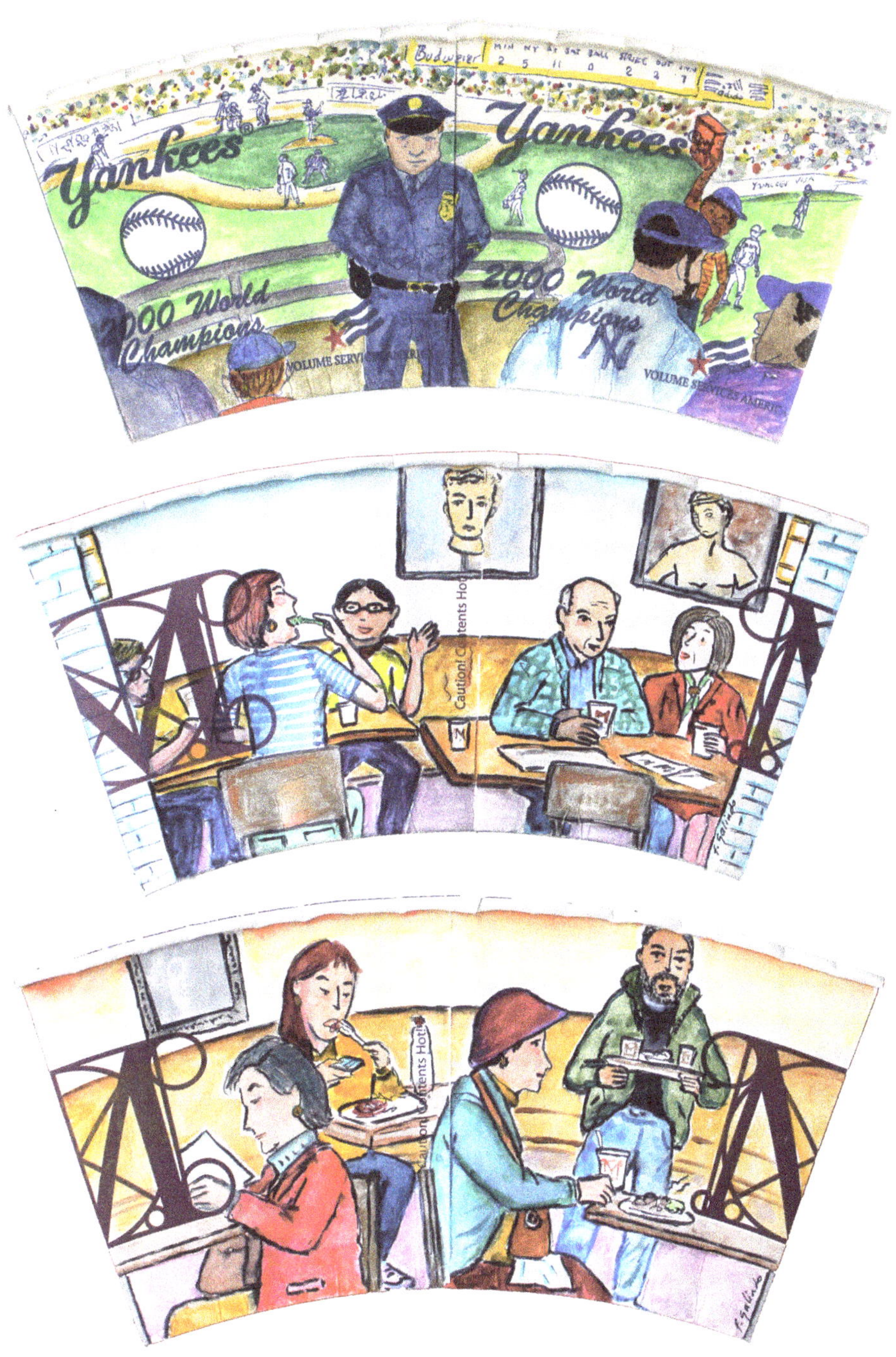
Yankees
2000 World Champions
Yankees
2000 World Champions

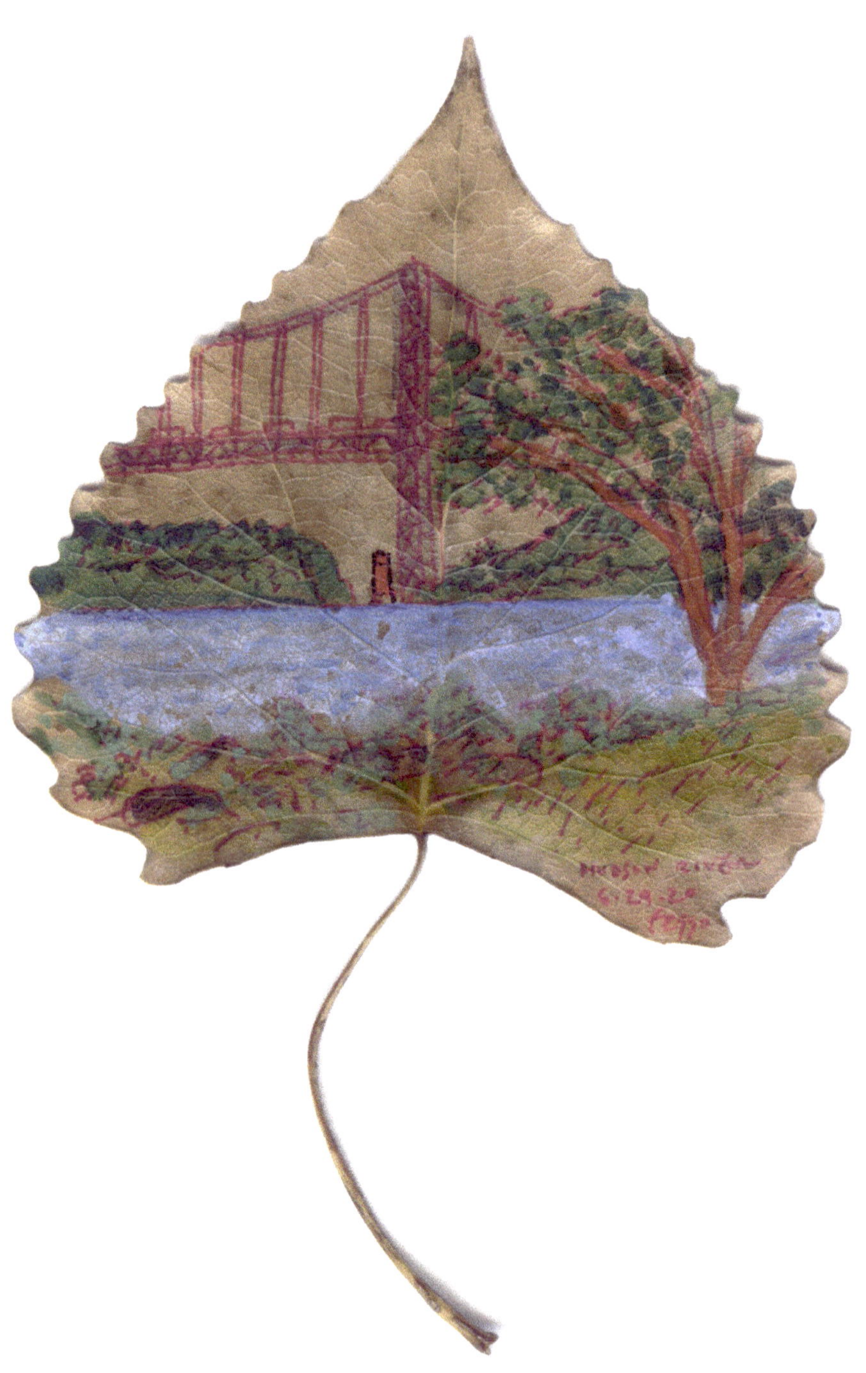
HUDSON RIVER
6.29.20

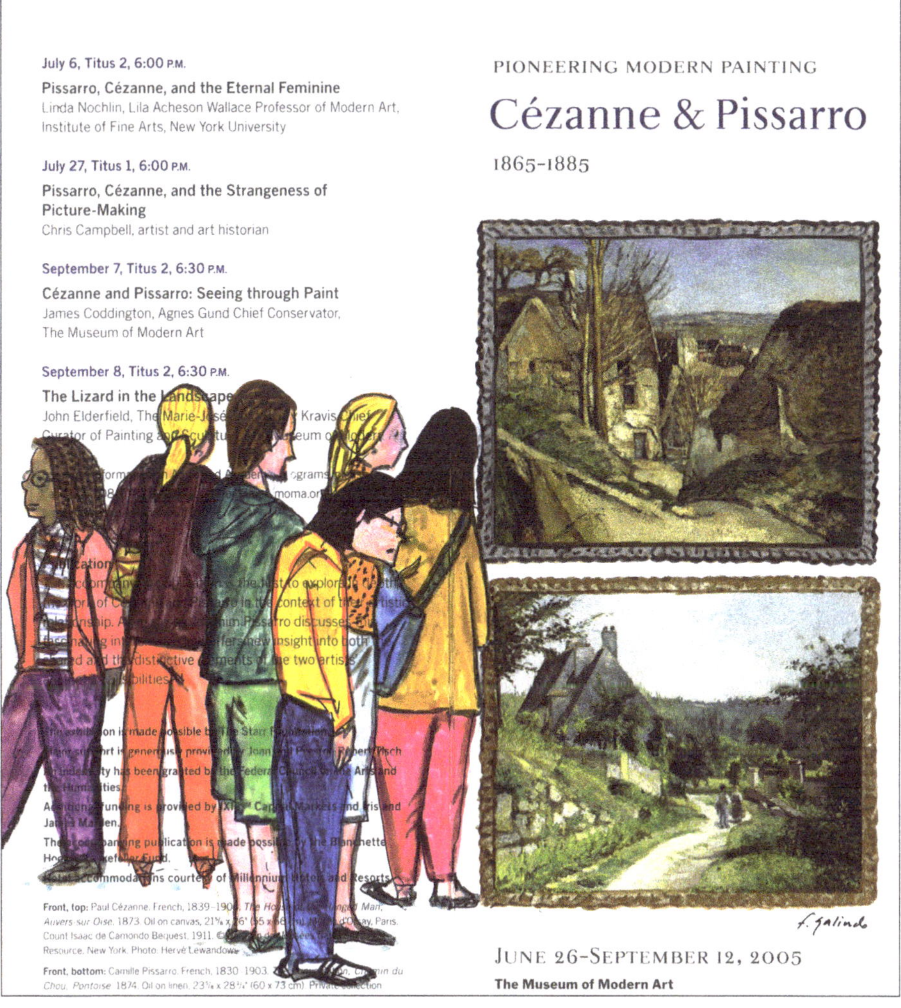
July 6, Titus 2, 6:00 P.M.
Pissarro, Cézanne, and the Eternal Feminine
Linda Nochlin, Lila Acheson Wallace Professor of Modern Art, Institute of Fine Arts, New York University
July 27, Titus 1, 6:00 P.M.
Pissarro, Cézanne, and the Strangeness of Picture-Making
Chris Campbell, artist and art historian
September 7, Titus 2, 6:30 P.M.
Cézanne and Pissarro: Seeing through Paint
James Coddington, Agnes Gund Chief Conservator, The Museum of Modern Art
September 8, Titus 2, 6:30 P.M.
PIONEERING MODERN PAINTING
Cézanne & Pissarro
1865–1885
f. galindo
JUNE 26–SEPTEMBER 12, 2005
The Museum of Modern Art

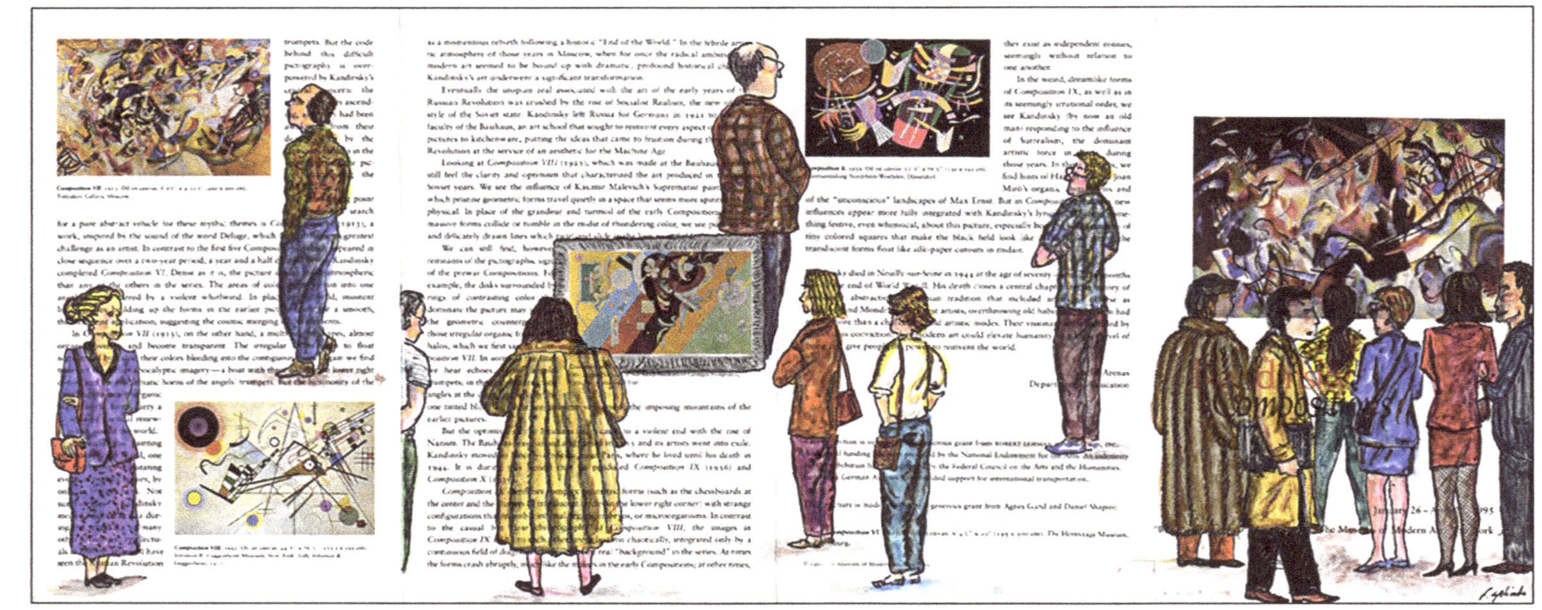

as a momentous rebirth following a historic "End of the World." In the febrile
tic atmosphere of those years in Moscow, when for once the radical ambitions of
modern art seemed to be bound up with dramatic, profound historical ch
Kandinsky's art underwent a significant transformation.
Eventually the utopian zeal associated with the art of the early years of
Russian Revolution was crushed by the rise of Socialist Realism, the new
style of the Soviet state. Kandinsky left Russia for Germany in 1922 to
faculty of the Bauhaus, an art school that sought to reinvent every aspect of
pictures to kitchenware, putting the ideas that came to fruition during th
Revolution at the service of an aesthetic for the Machine Age.
Looking at Composition VIII (1923), which was made at the Bauhaus
still feel the clarity and optimism that characterized the art produced in
Soviet years. We see the influence of Kasimir Malevich's Suprematist pain
which pristine geometric forms travel quietly in a space that seems more spirit
physical. In place of the grandeur and turmoil of the early Compositions
massive forms collide or tumble in the midst of thundering color, we see p
and delicately drawn lines which
the imposing mountains of the
earlier pictures.
to a violent end with the rise of
Nazism. The Bauh
and its artists went into exile.
Kandinsky moved
where he lived until his death in
1944. It is dur
Composition IX (1936) and
Composition X
forms (such as the chessboards at
the center and the
the lower right corner) with strange
configurations th
or microorganisms. In contrast
to the casual
Composition VIII, the images in
Composition IX
chaotically, integrated only by a
continuous field of diag
real "background" in the series. At times
the forms crash abruptly,
in the early Compositions; at other times,
of the "unconscious" landscapes of Max Ernst. But in Compo
influences appear more fully integrated with Kandinsky's
thing festive, even whimsical, about this picture, especially
tiny colored squares that make the black field look like
translucent forms float like silk-paper cutouts in midair.
they exist as independent entities,
seemingly without relation to
one another.
In the weird, dreamlike forms
of Composition IX, as well as in
its seemingly irrational order, we
see Kandinsky (by now an old
man) responding to the influence
of Surrealism, the dominant
artistic force in
during
those years.
find hints of
Miró's organ
died in Neuilly-sur-Seine in 1944 at the age of seventy
end of World War II. His death closes a central chapt
give people
to reinvent the world.

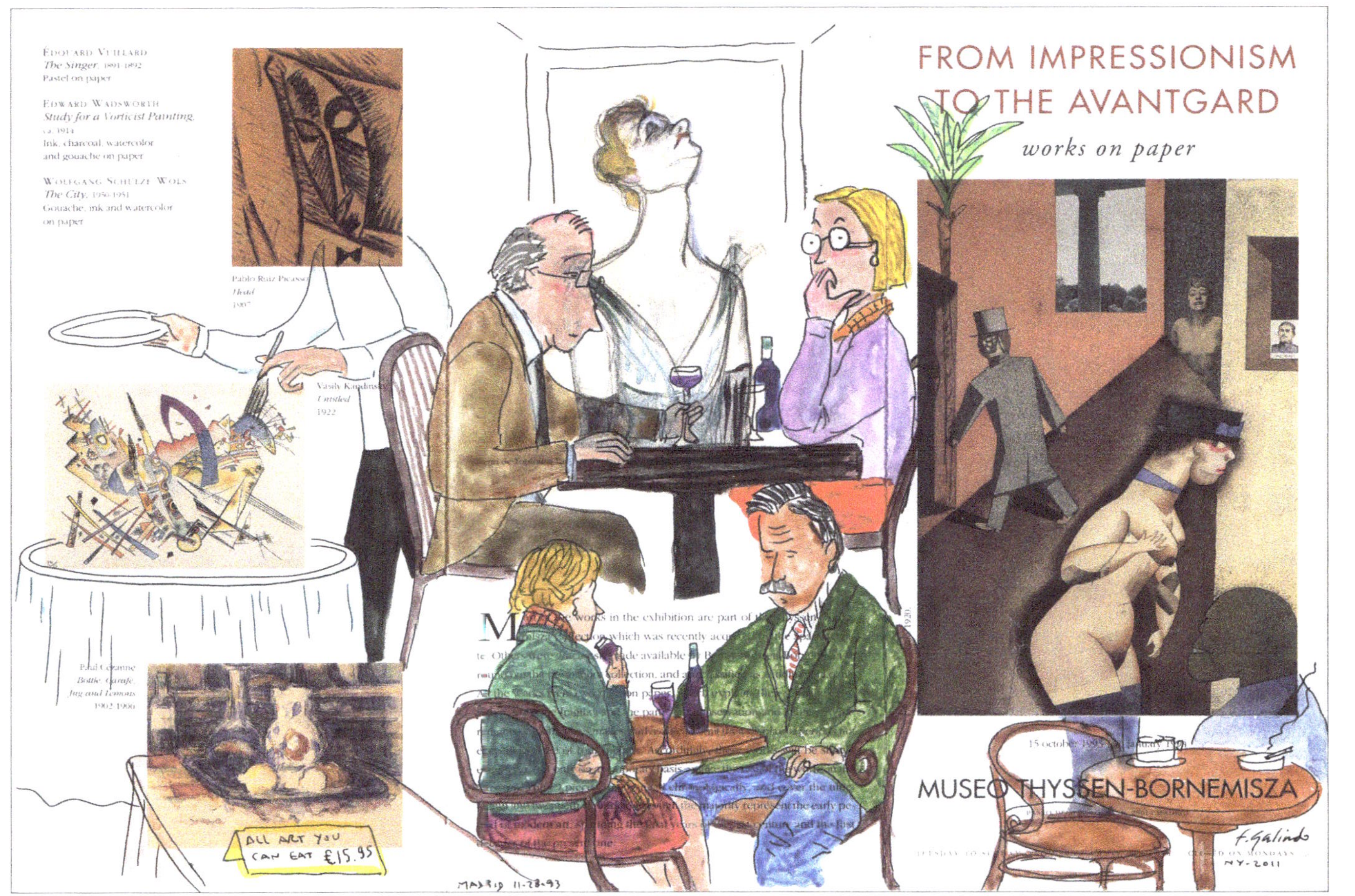
FROM IMPRESSIONISM
TO THE AVANTGARD
works on paper
Edouard Vuillard
The Singer, 1891-1892
Pastel on paper
Edward Wadsworth
Study for a Vorticist Painting,
ca. 1914
Ink, charcoal, watercolor
and gouache on paper
Wolfgang Schulze Wols
The City, 1950-1951
Gouache, ink and watercolor
on paper
Pablo Ruiz Picasso
Head
1907
Vasily Kandinsky
Untitled
1922
Paul Cézanne
Bottle, Carafe,
Jug and Lemons
1902-1906
ALL ART YOU
CAN EAT £15.95
MUSEO THYSSEN-BORNEMISZA
MADRID 11-28-93
F. Galindo
NY-2011

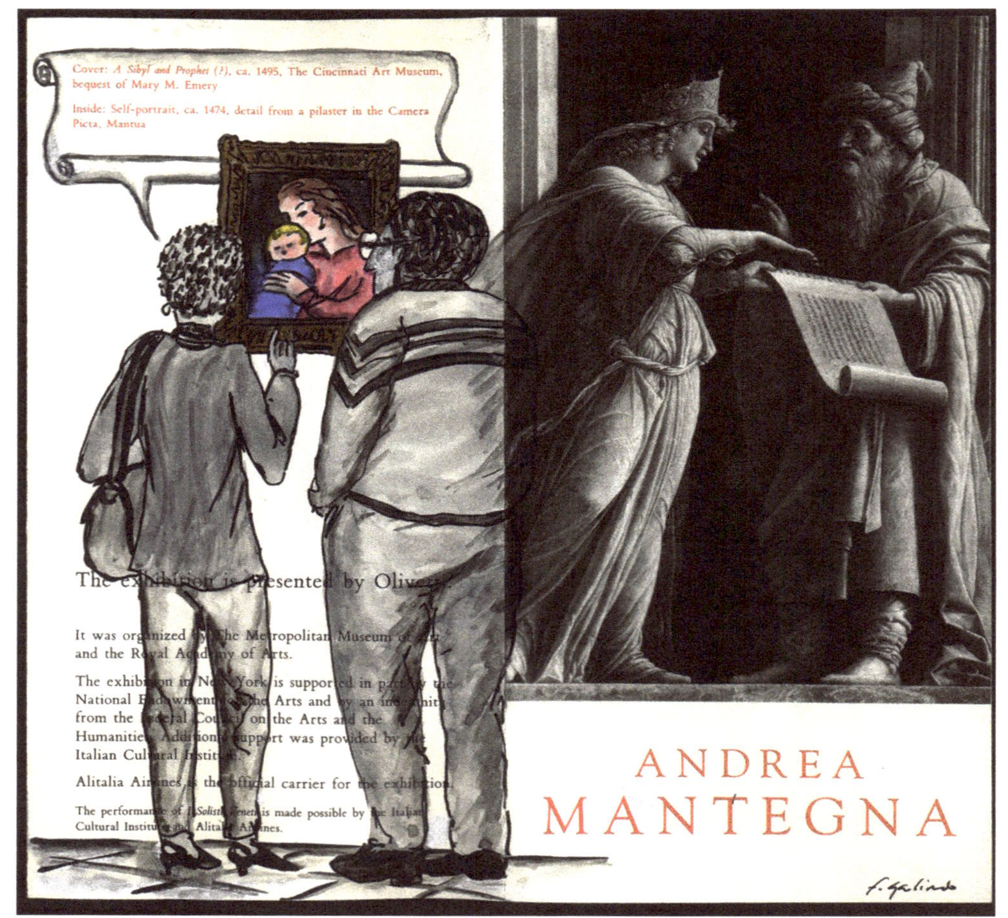
Cover: *A Sibyl and Prophet (?)*, ca. 1495, The Cincinnati Art Museum, bequest of Mary M. Emery
Inside: Self-portrait, ca. 1474, detail from a pilaster in the Camera Picta, Mantua
The exhibition is presented by Olive
It was organized by The Metropolitan Museum of and the Royal Academy of Arts.
The exhibition in New York is supported in part by the National Endowment for the Arts and by an indemnity from the Federal Council on the Arts and the Humanities. Additional support was provided by the Italian Cultural Institute.
Alitalia Airlines is the official carrier for the exhibition.
The performance of I Solisti Veneti is made possible by the Italian Cultural Institute and Alitalia Airlines.
ANDREA
MANTEGNA

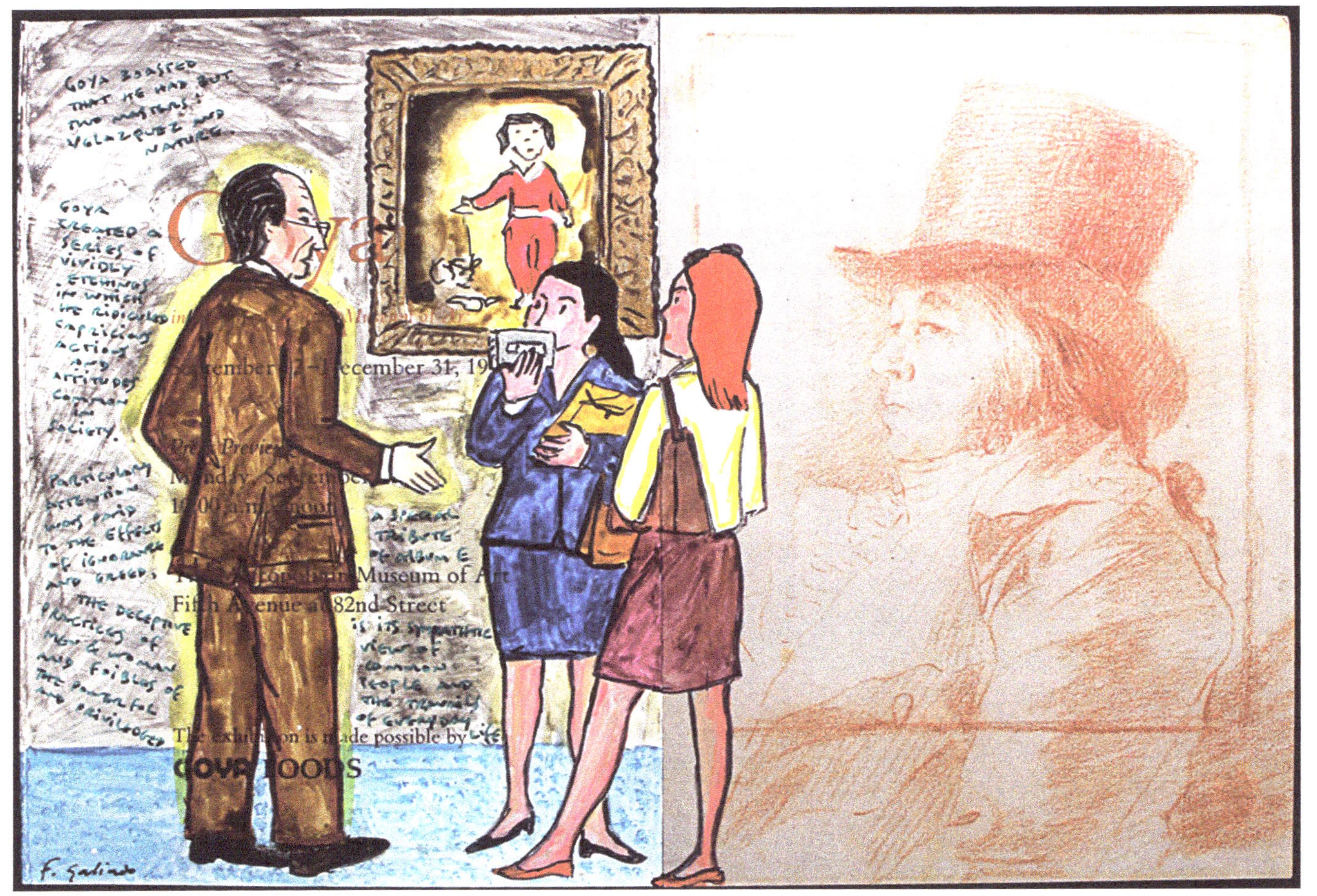
GOYA BOASTED THAT HE HAD BUT TWO MASTERS: VELAZQUEZ AND NATURE.
GOYA CREATED A SERIES OF VIVIDLY ETCHINGS IN WHICH HE RIDICULED CAPRICIOUS ACTIONS AND ATTITUDES COMMON IN SOCIETY.
PARTICULARLY ATTENTION WAS PAID TO THE EFFECTS OF IGNORANCE AND GREED, THE DECEPTIVE PRACTICES OF MEN & WOMEN AND FOIBLES OF THE POWERFUL AND PRIVILEGED
Goya
Museum of Art
Fifth Avenue at 82nd Street
F. Galindo

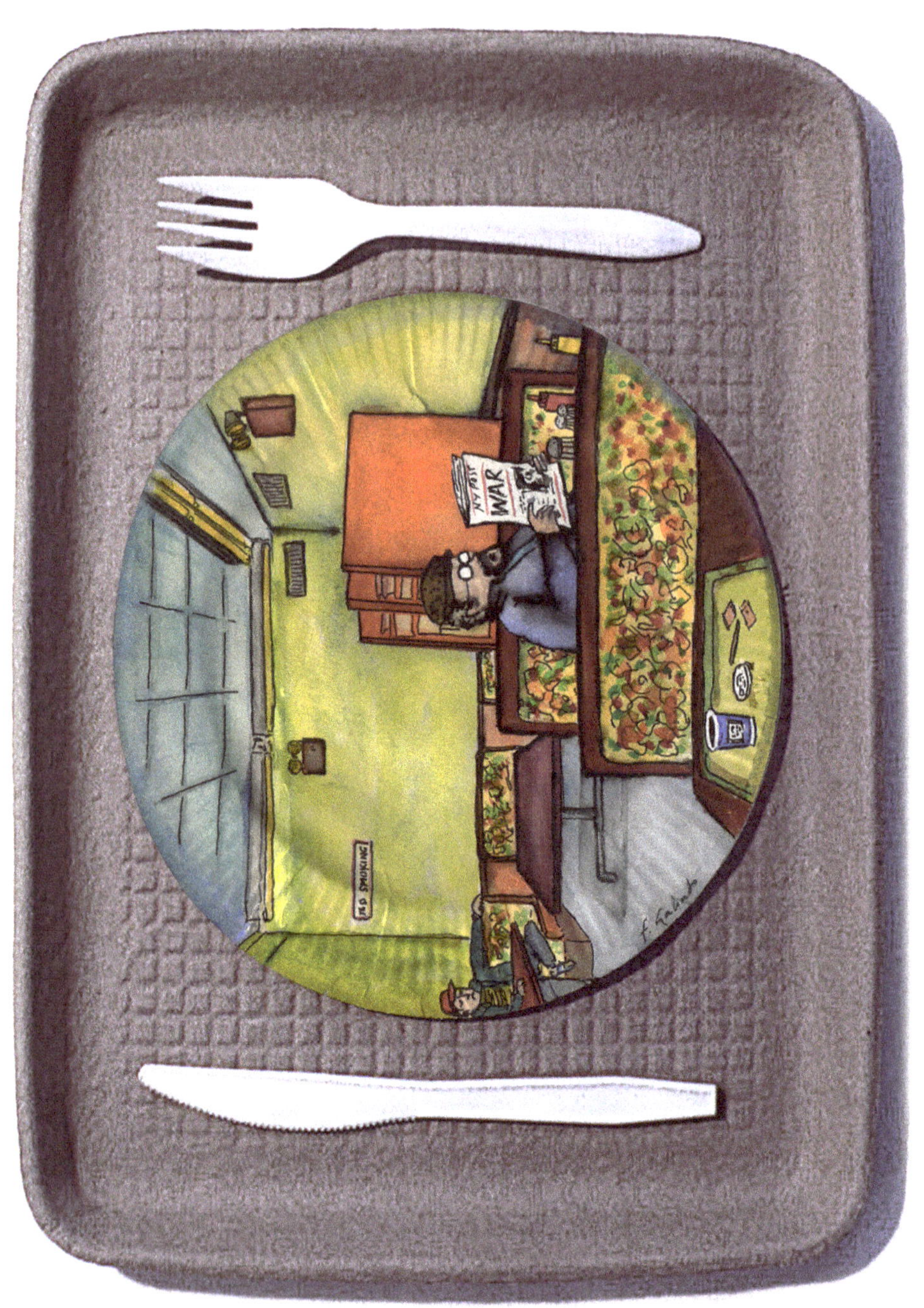
NY POST
WAR

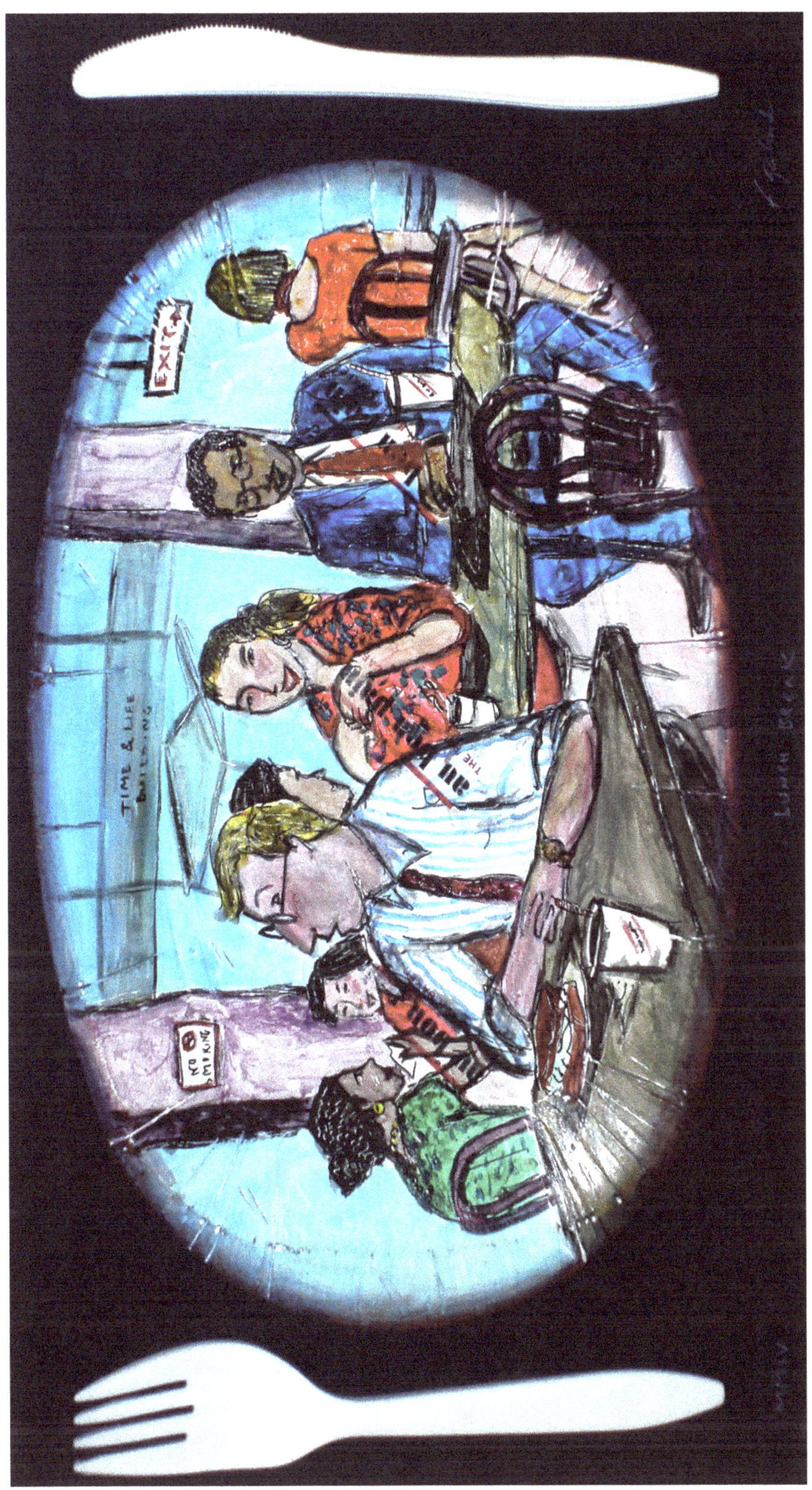
TIME & LIFE BUILDING
EXIT
NO SMOKING
LUNCH BREAK

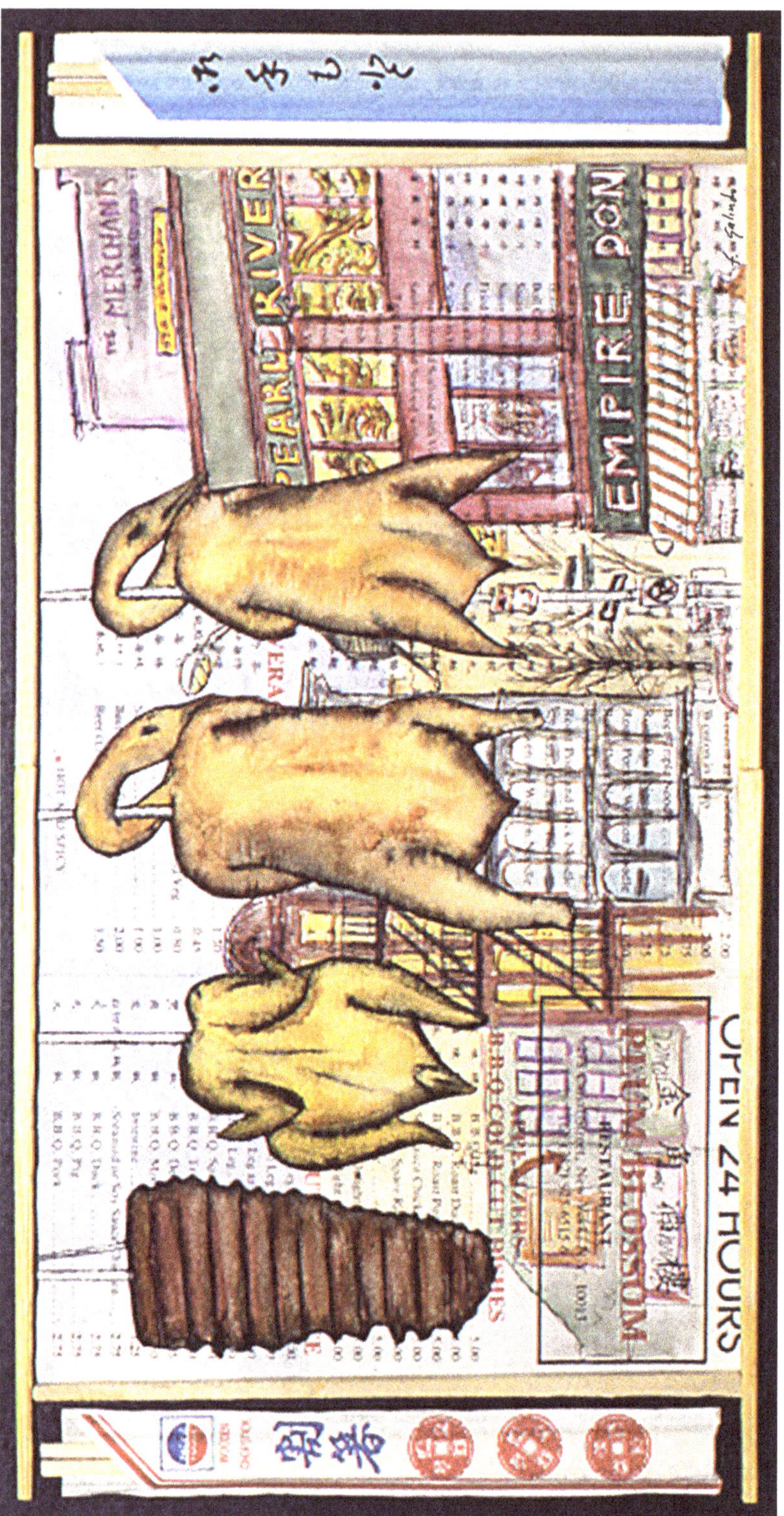

MERCHANTS
PEARL RIVER
EMPIRE DON
OPEN 24 HOURS
PLUM BLOSSOM
RESTAURANT
B-B-Q COLD CUT DISHES

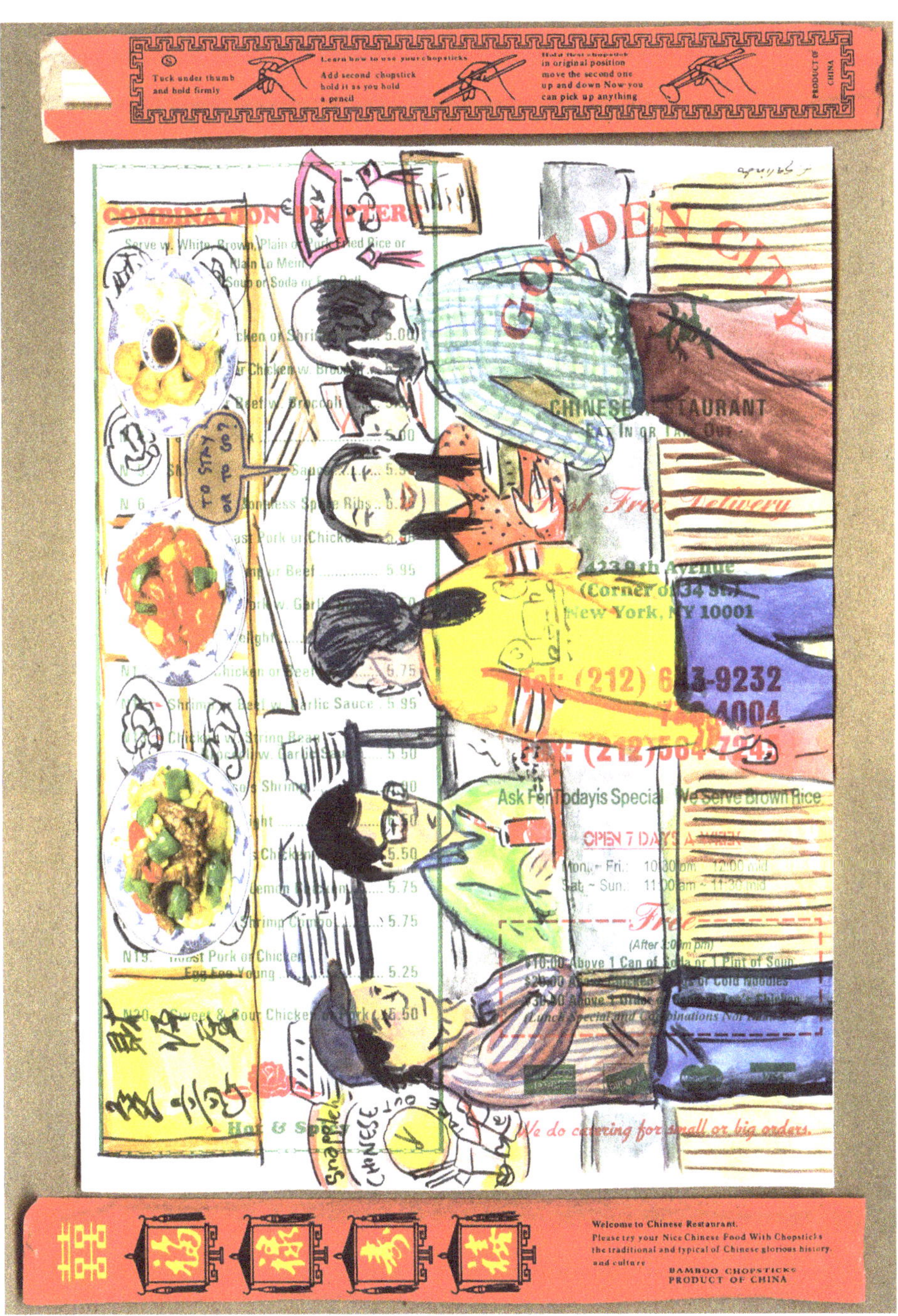
Tuck under thumb and hold firmly
Learn how to use your chopsticks
Add second chopstick hold it as you hold a pencil
in original position move the second one up and down Now you can pick up anything
PRODUCT OF CHINA
Welcome to Chinese Restaurant.
Please try your Nice Chinese Food With Chopsticks the traditional and typical of Chinese glorious history and culture
BAMBOO CHOPSTICKS PRODUCT OF CHINA

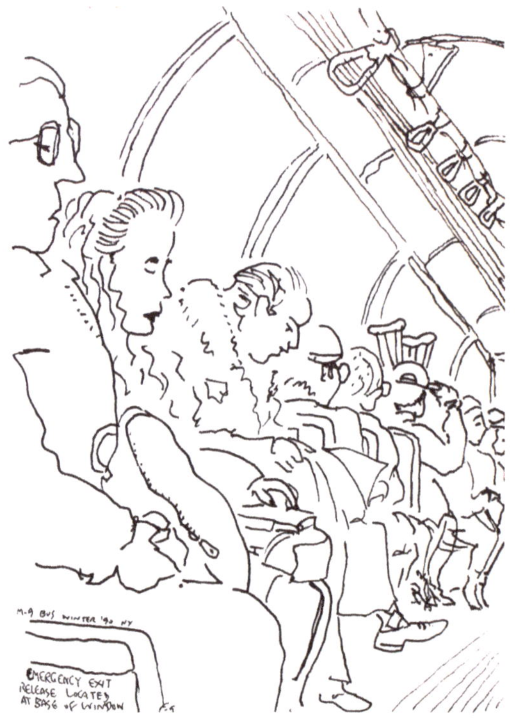
M-9 BUS WINTER '90 NY
EMERGENCY EXIT
RELEASE LOCATED
AT BASE OF WINDOW

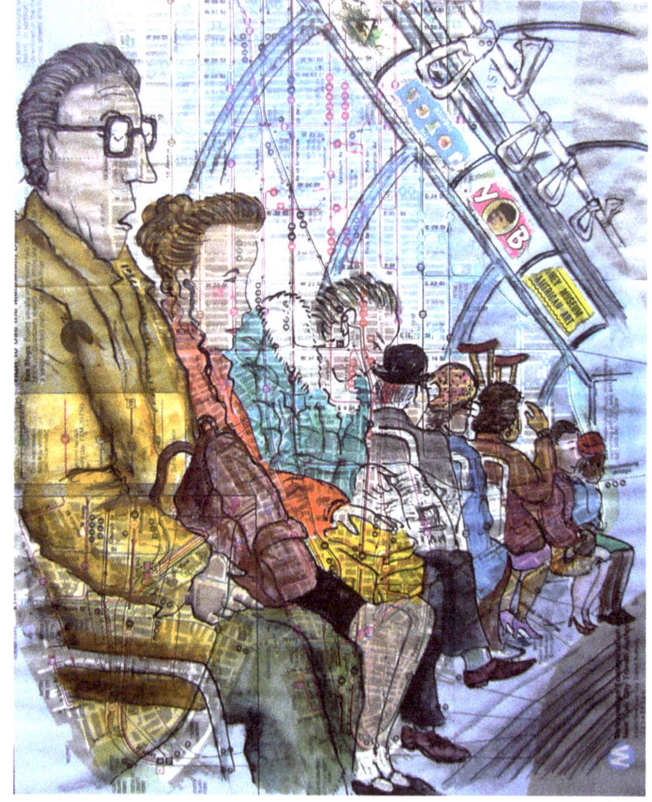
YOB

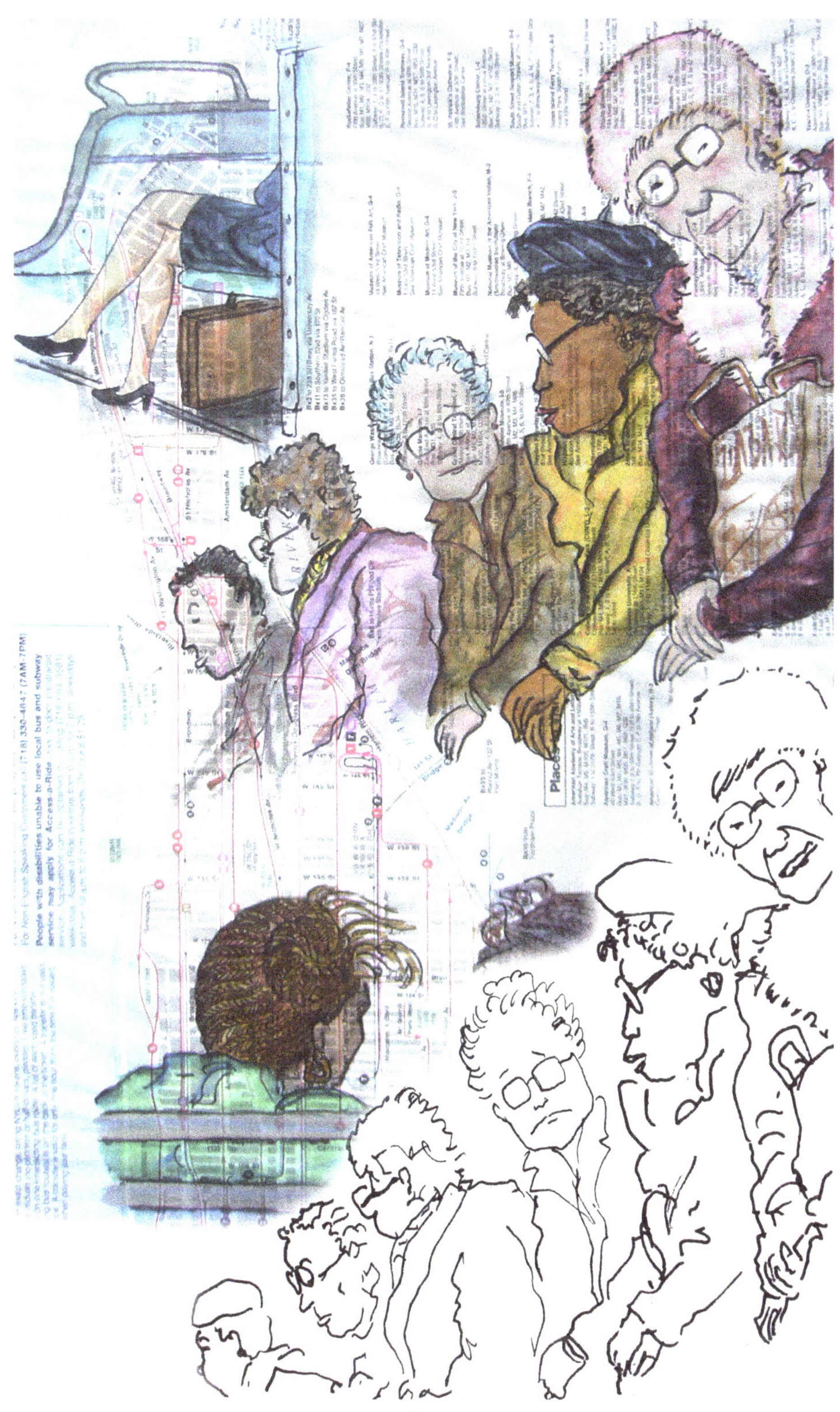

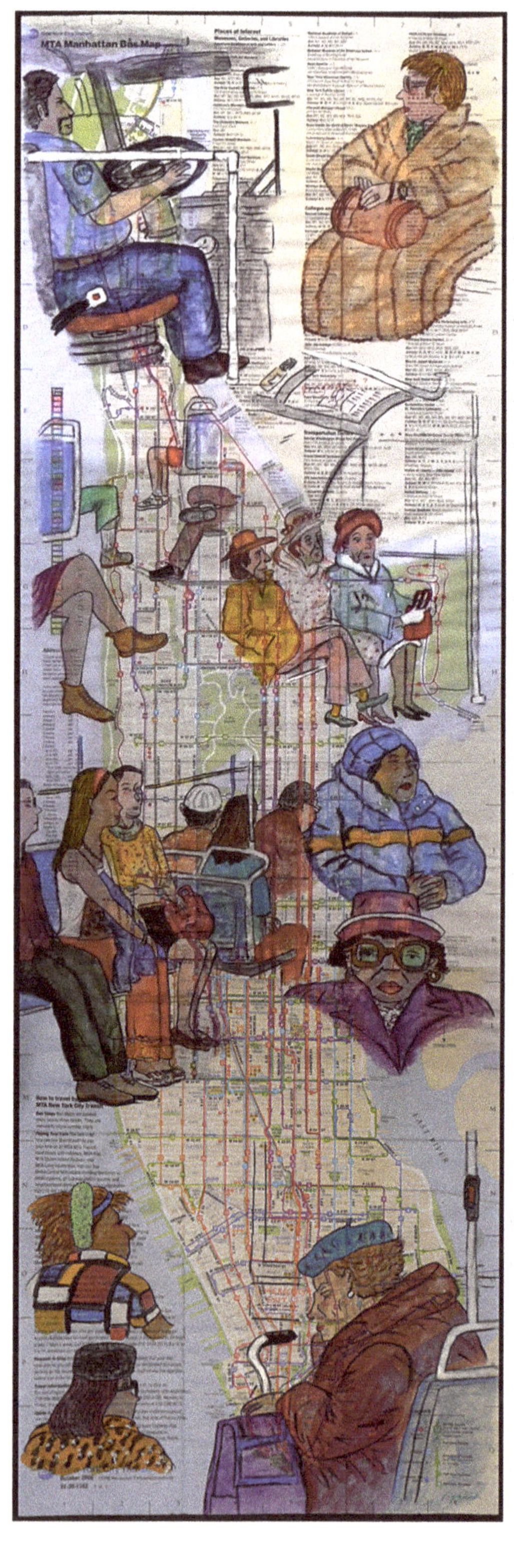
MTA Manhattan Bus Map

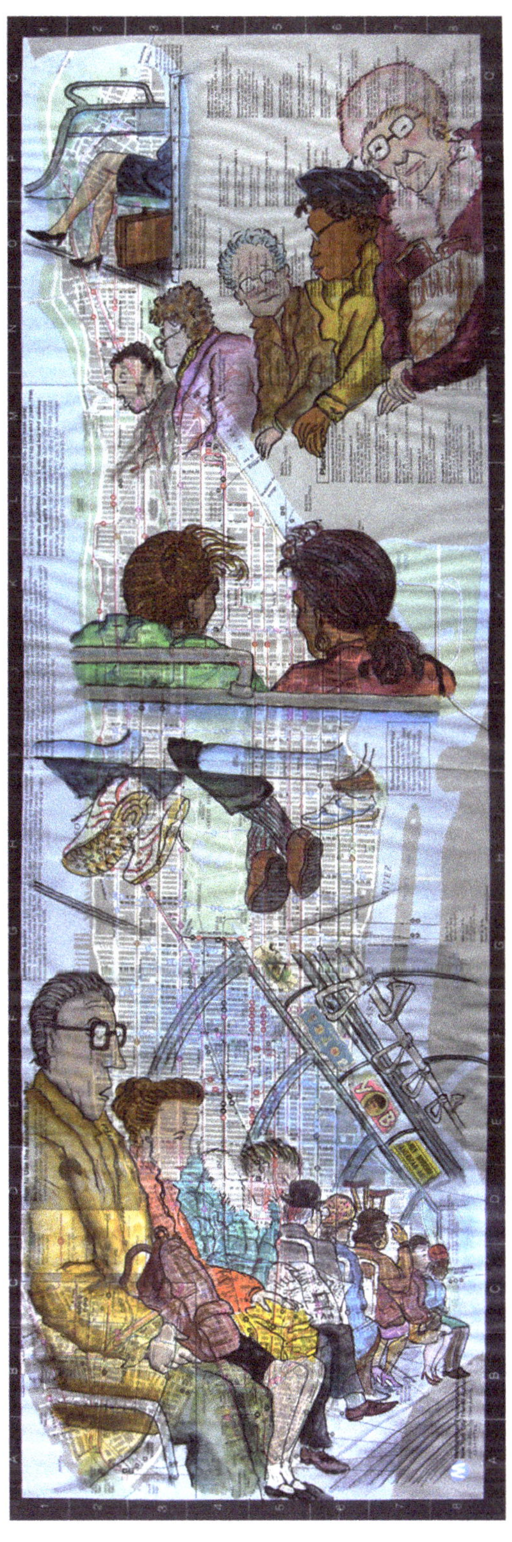

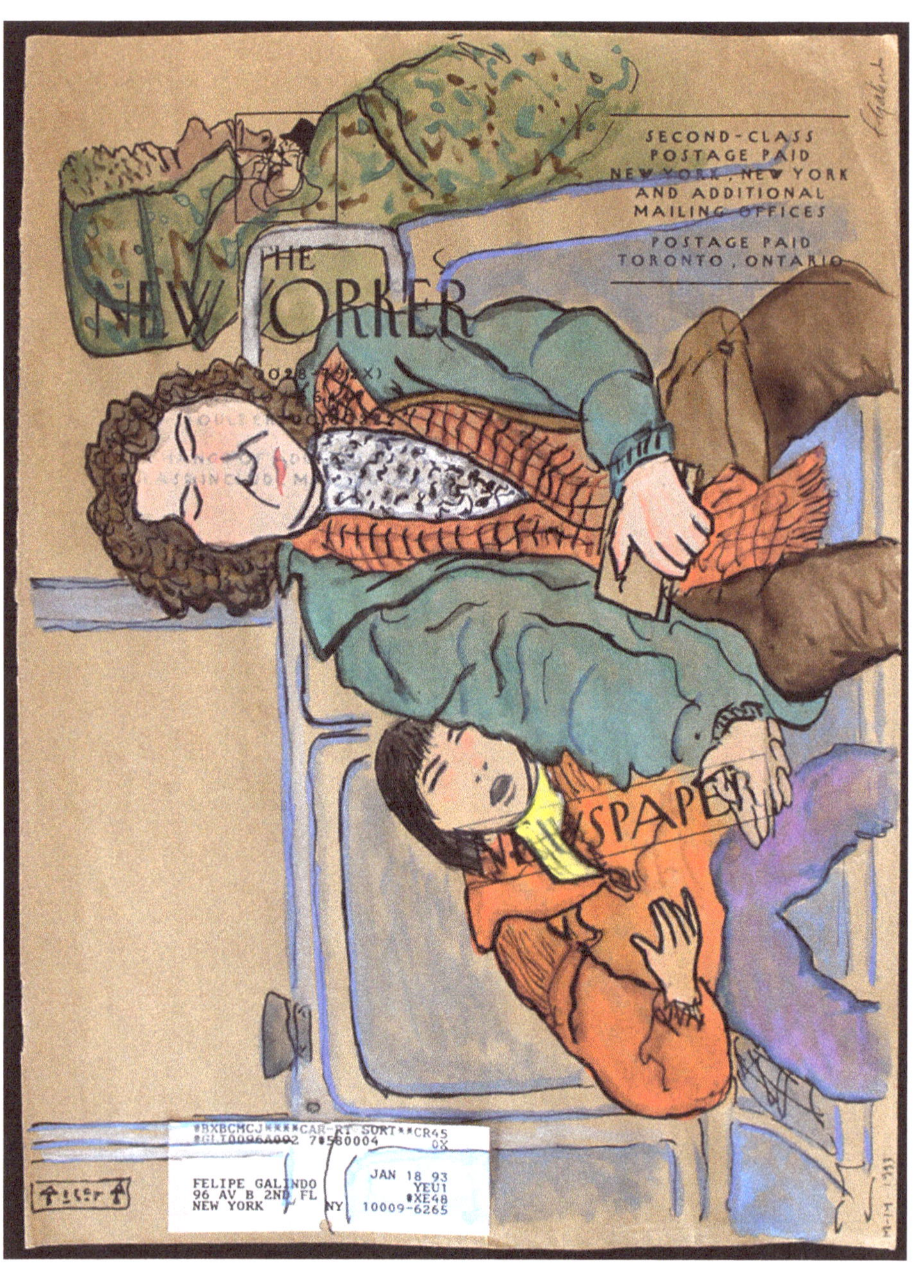
SECOND-CLASS
POSTAGE PAID
NEW YORK, NEW YORK
AND ADDITIONAL
MAILING OFFICES
POSTAGE PAID
TORONTO, ONTARIO
THE
NEW YORKER
NEWSPAPER
FELIPE GALINDO
96 AV B 2ND FL
NEW YORK NY
JAN 18 93
10009-6265

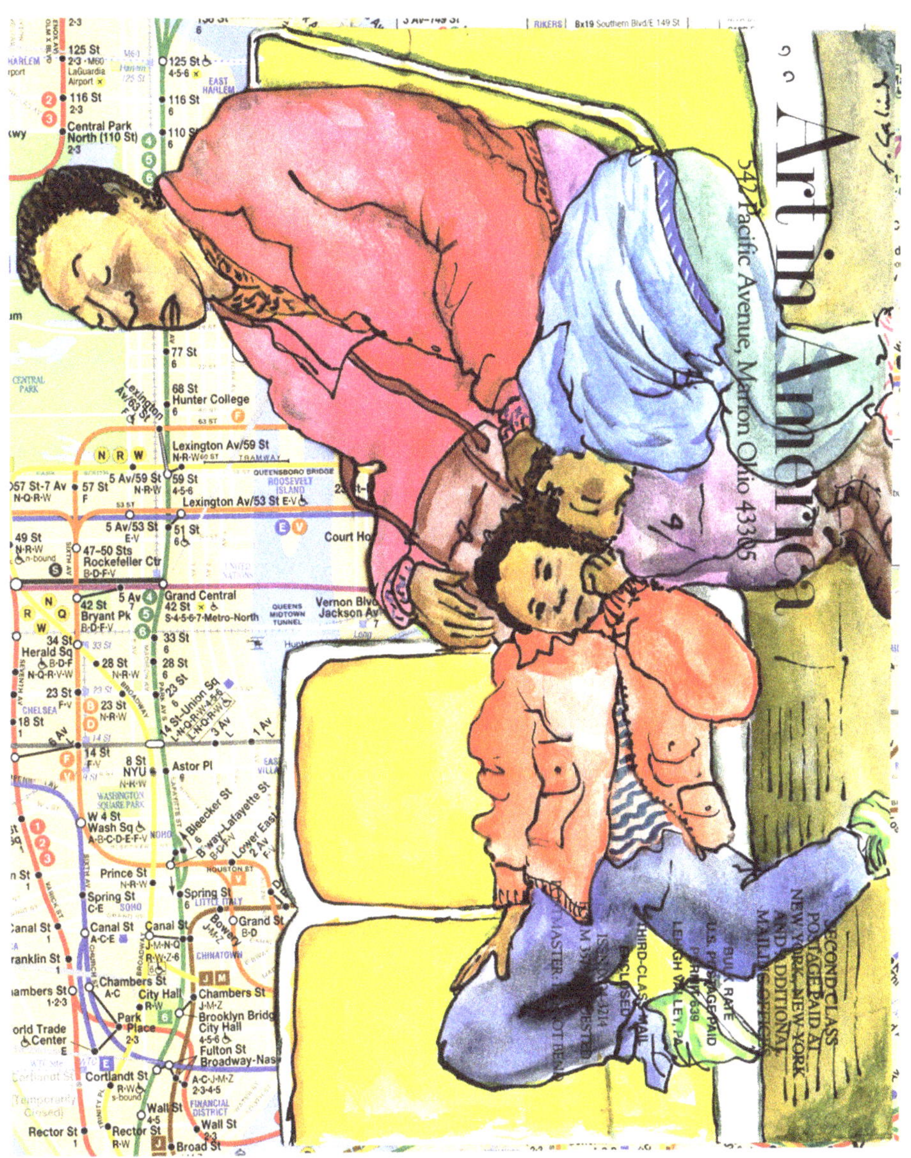
Art in America
547 Pacific Avenue, Marion Ohio 43305

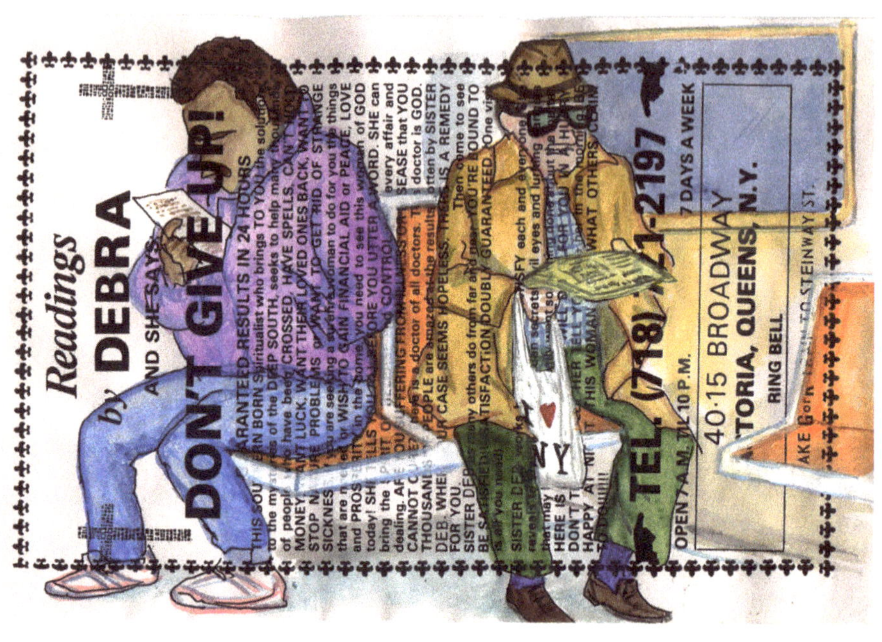
Readings
by DEBRA
AND SHE SAYS:
DON'T GIVE UP!
TEL. (718)
OPEN 7 A.M. TIL 10 P.M.
7 DAYS A WEEK
40-15 BROADWAY
TORIA, QUEENS, N.Y.
RING BELL

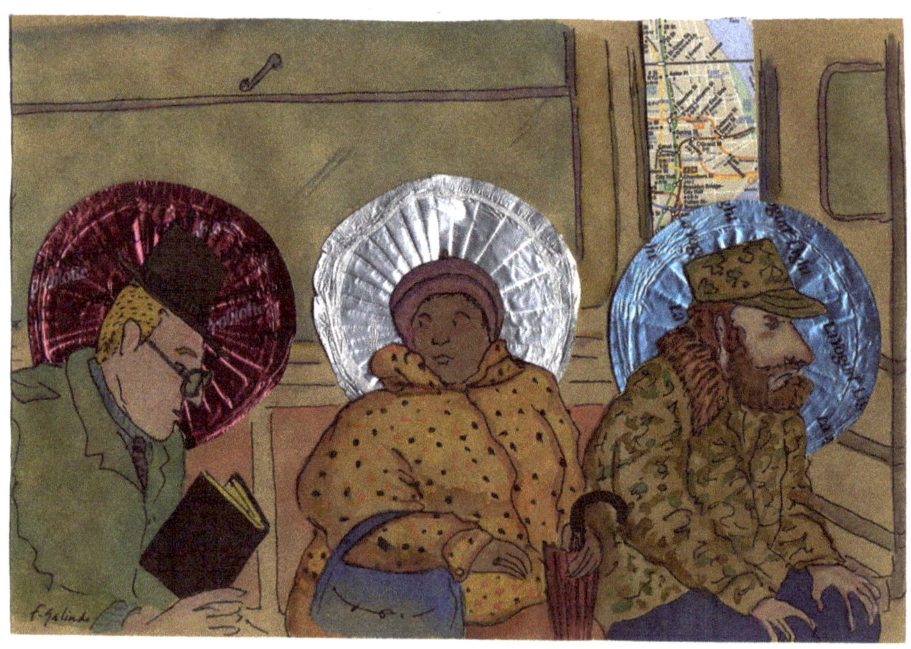

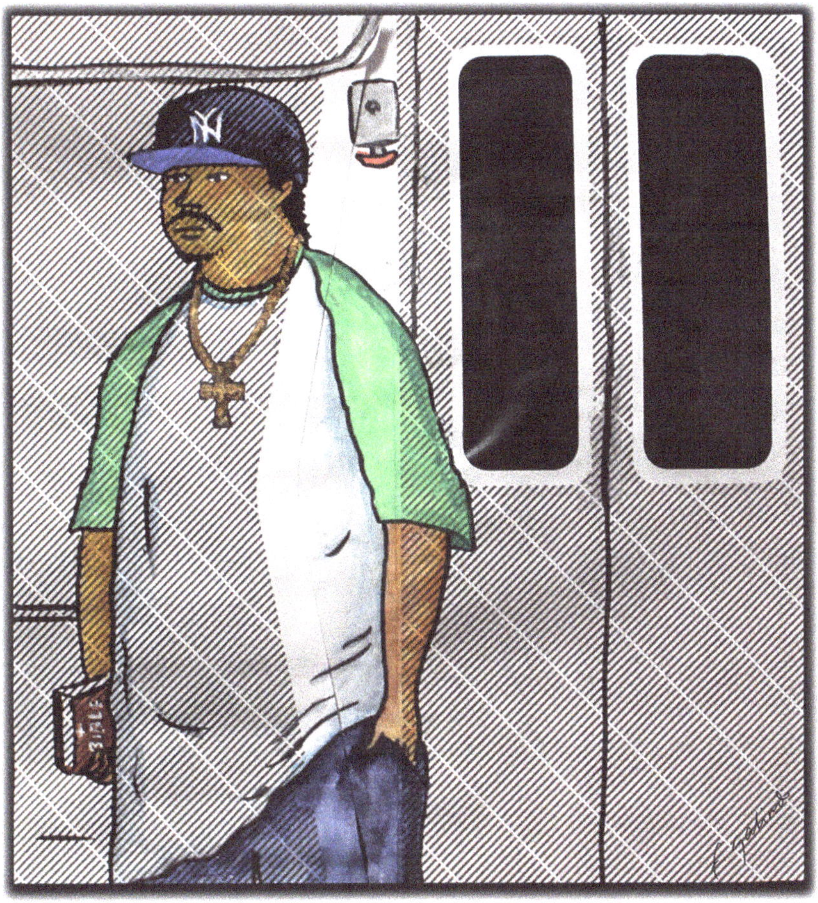

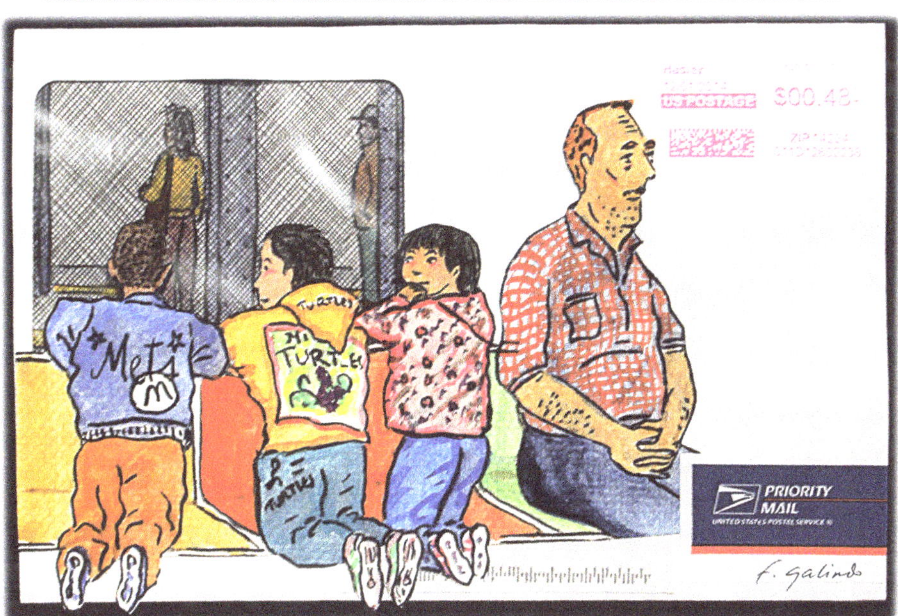
Mets
US POSTAGE
$00.48
PRIORITY
MAIL
UNITED STATES POSTAL SERVICE ®
F. Galindo

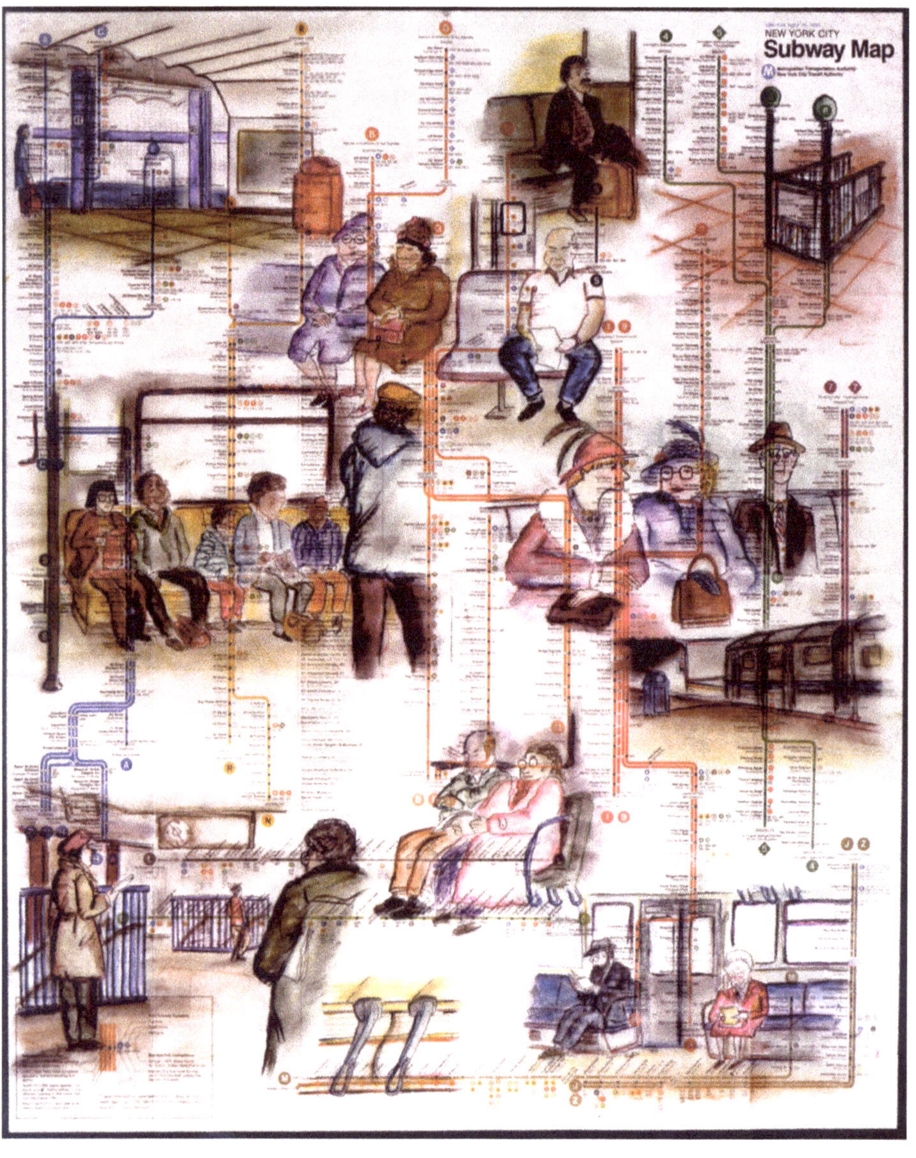
NEW YORK CITY
Subway Map

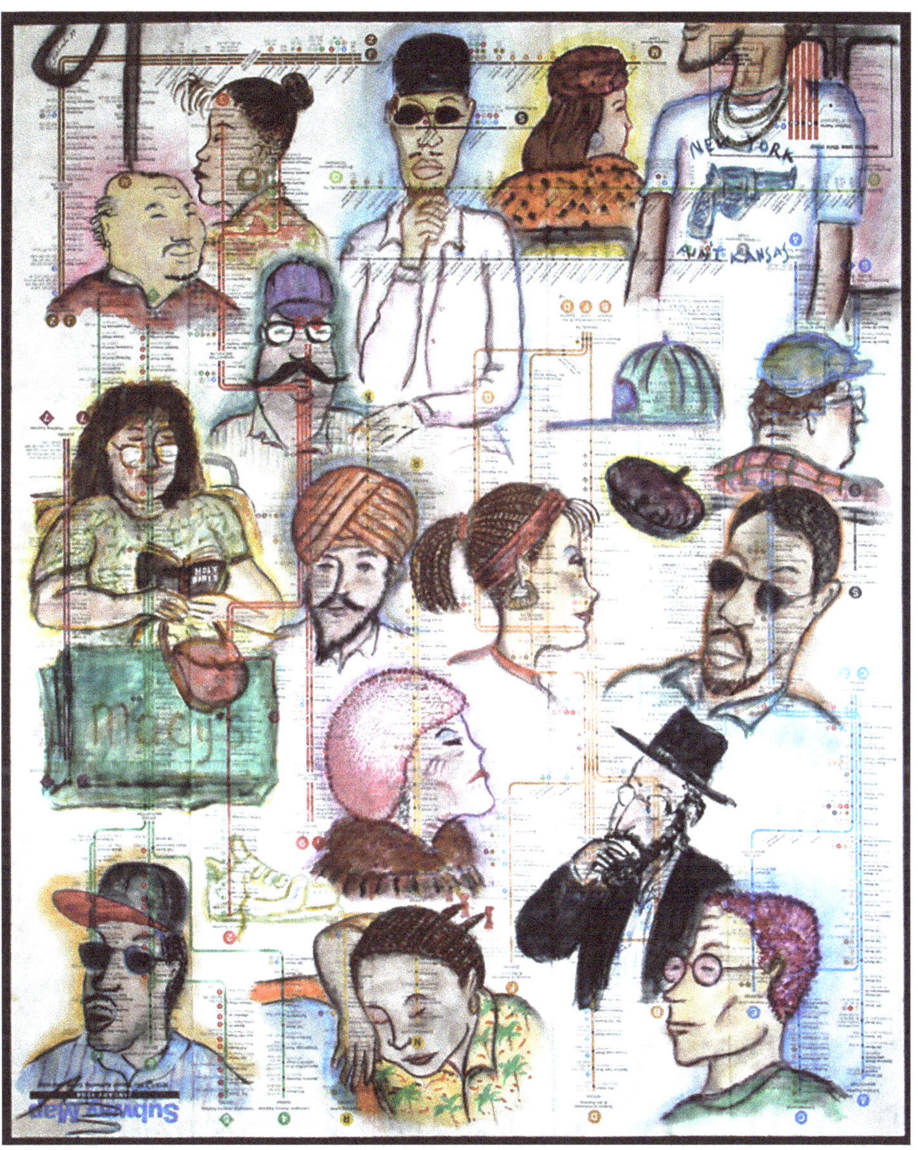
NEW YORK
AUNT KANSAS

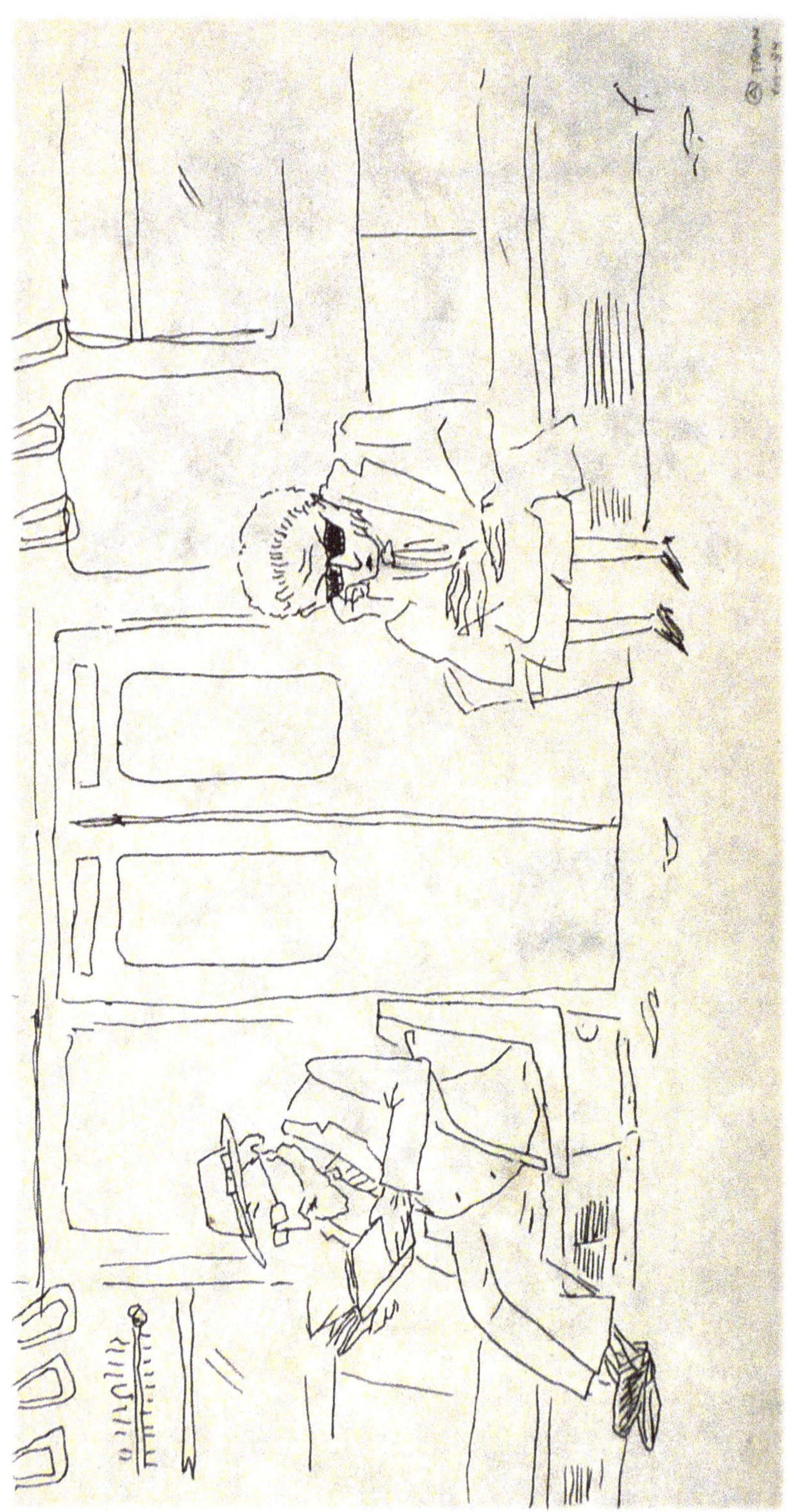

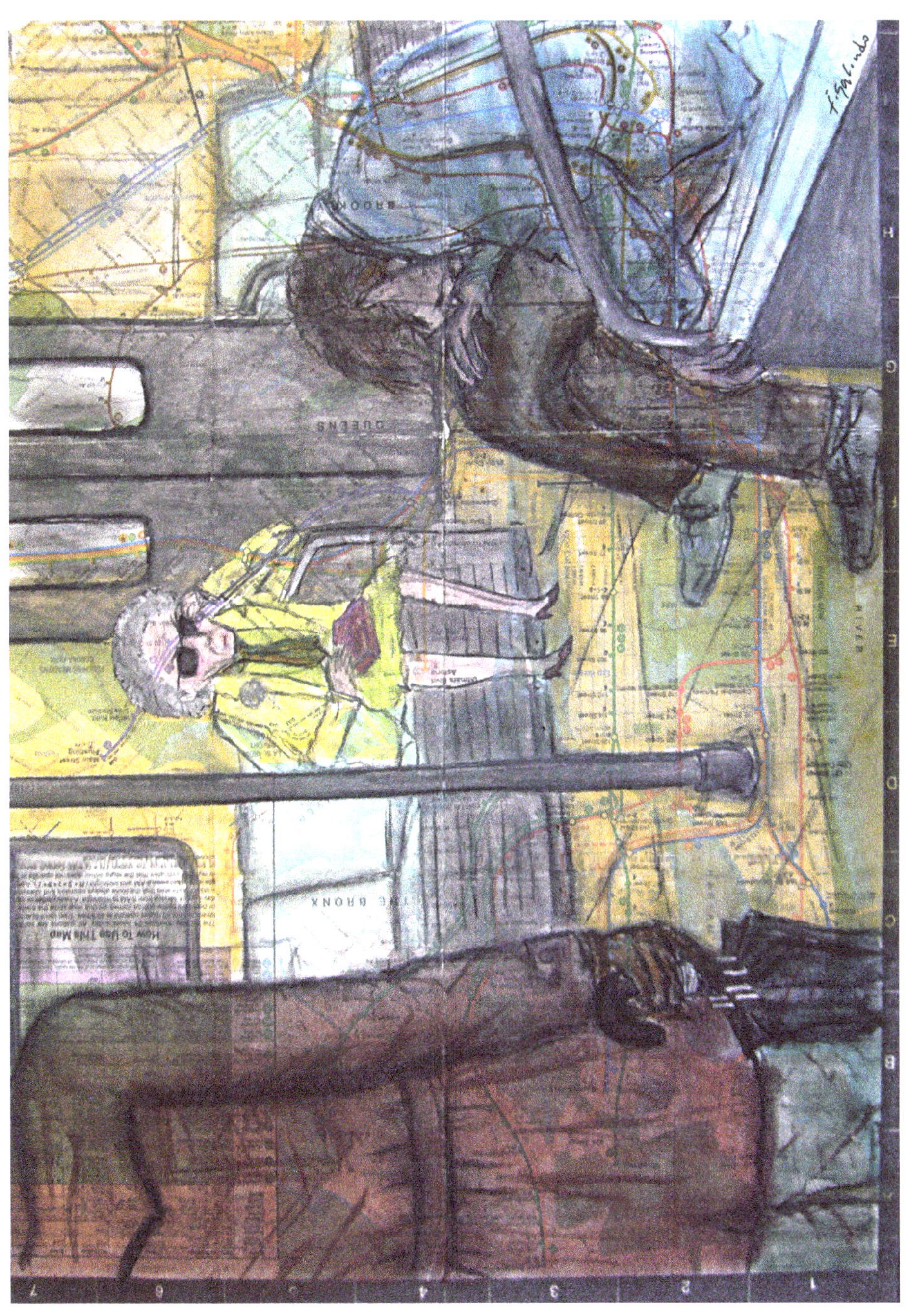
How to Use This Map
THE BRONX
QUEENS

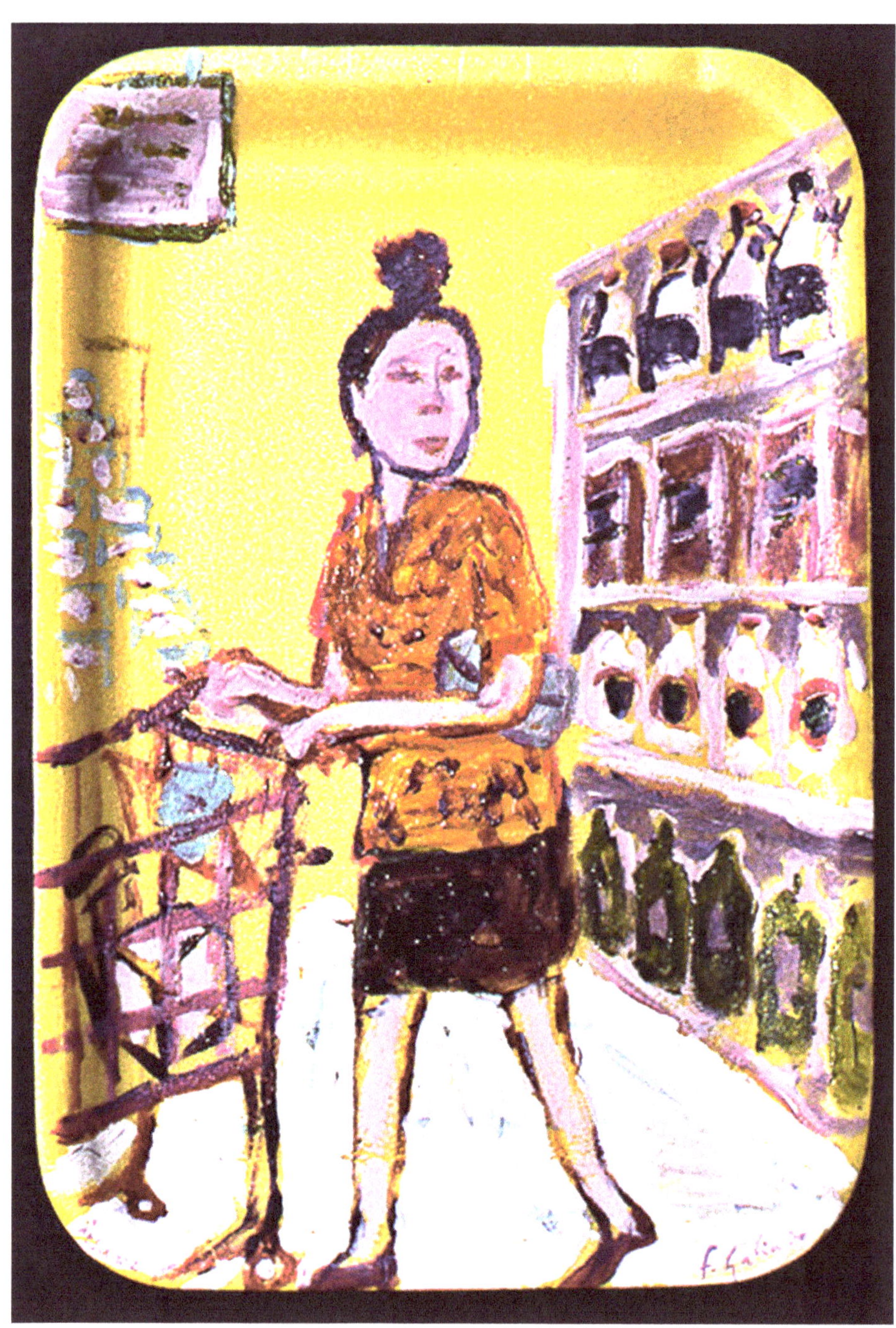

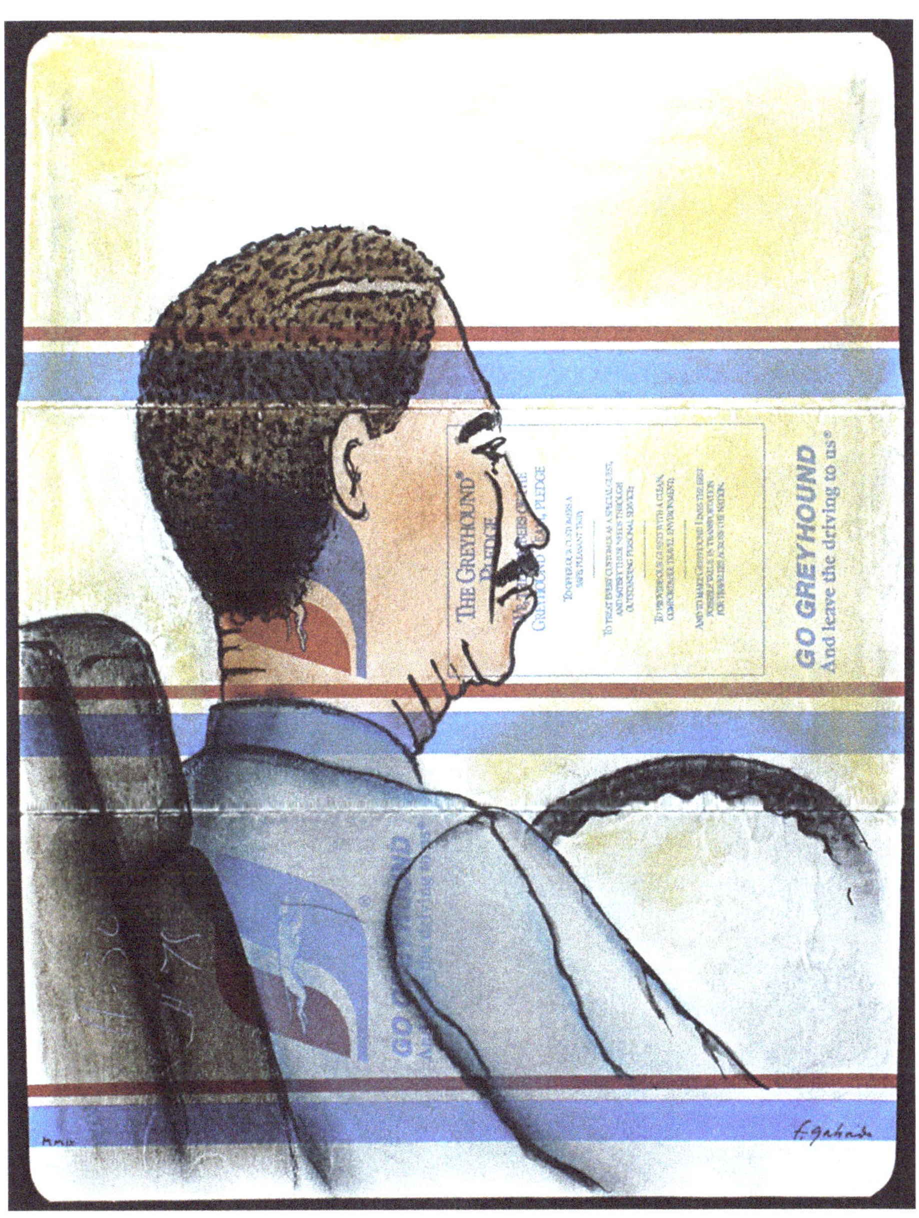
The Greyhound®
Pledge
GO GREYHOUND
And leave the driving to us®

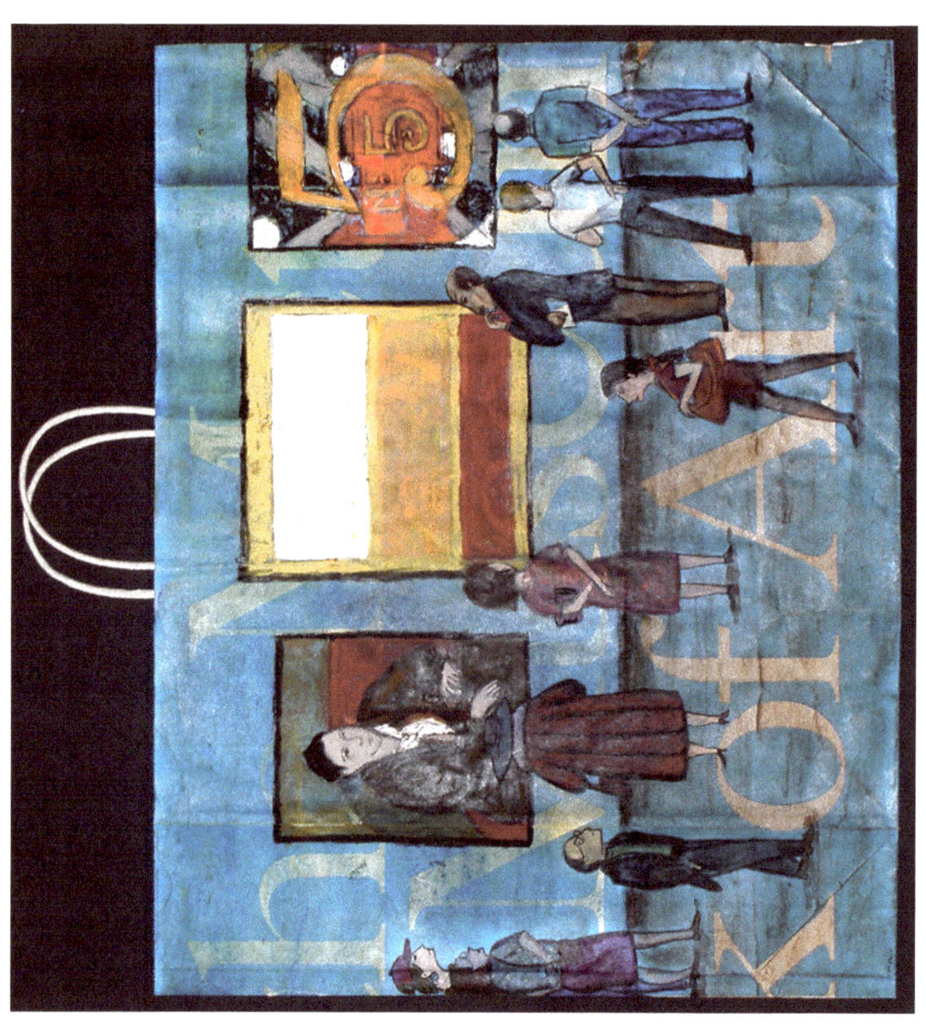

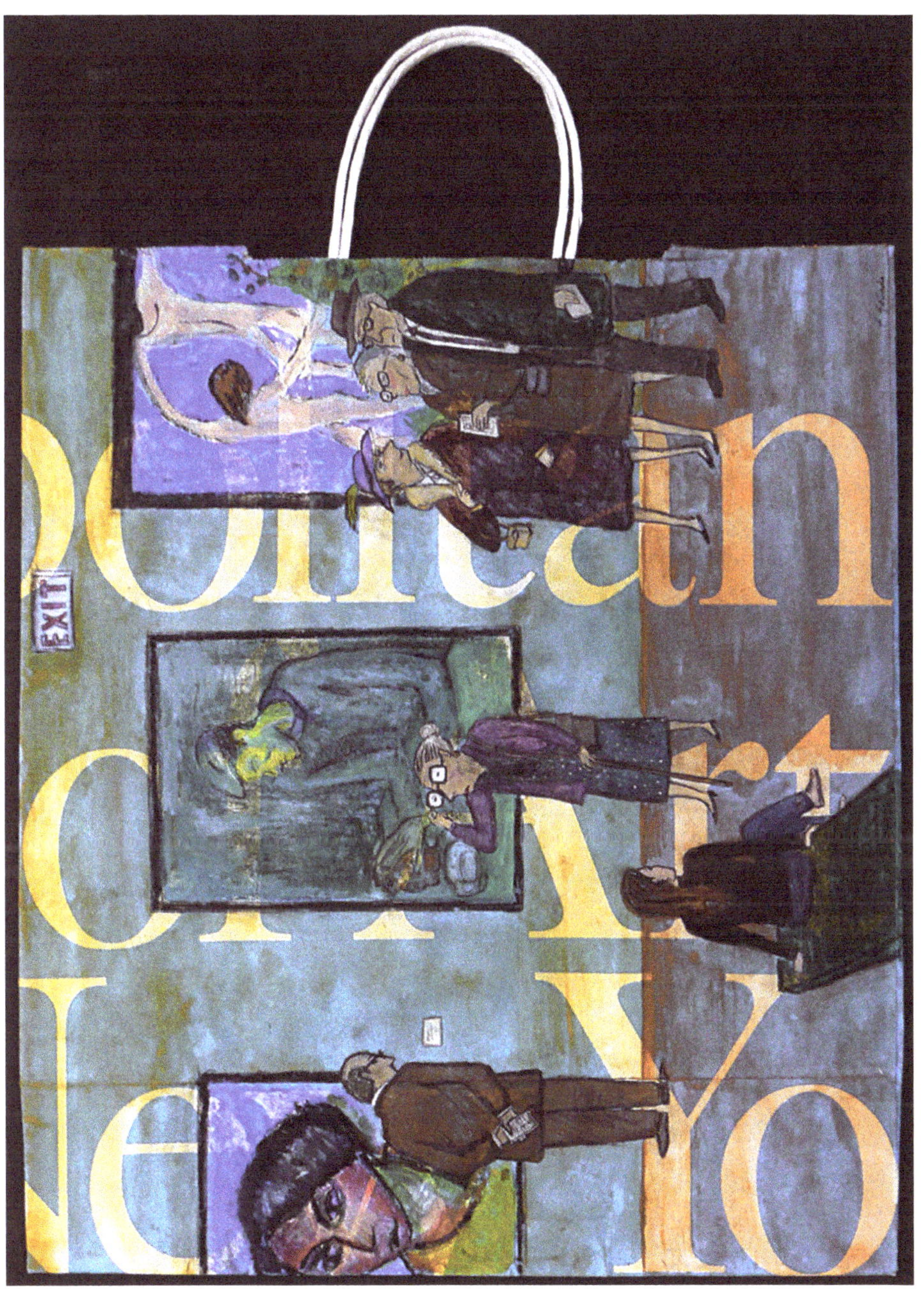
EXIT

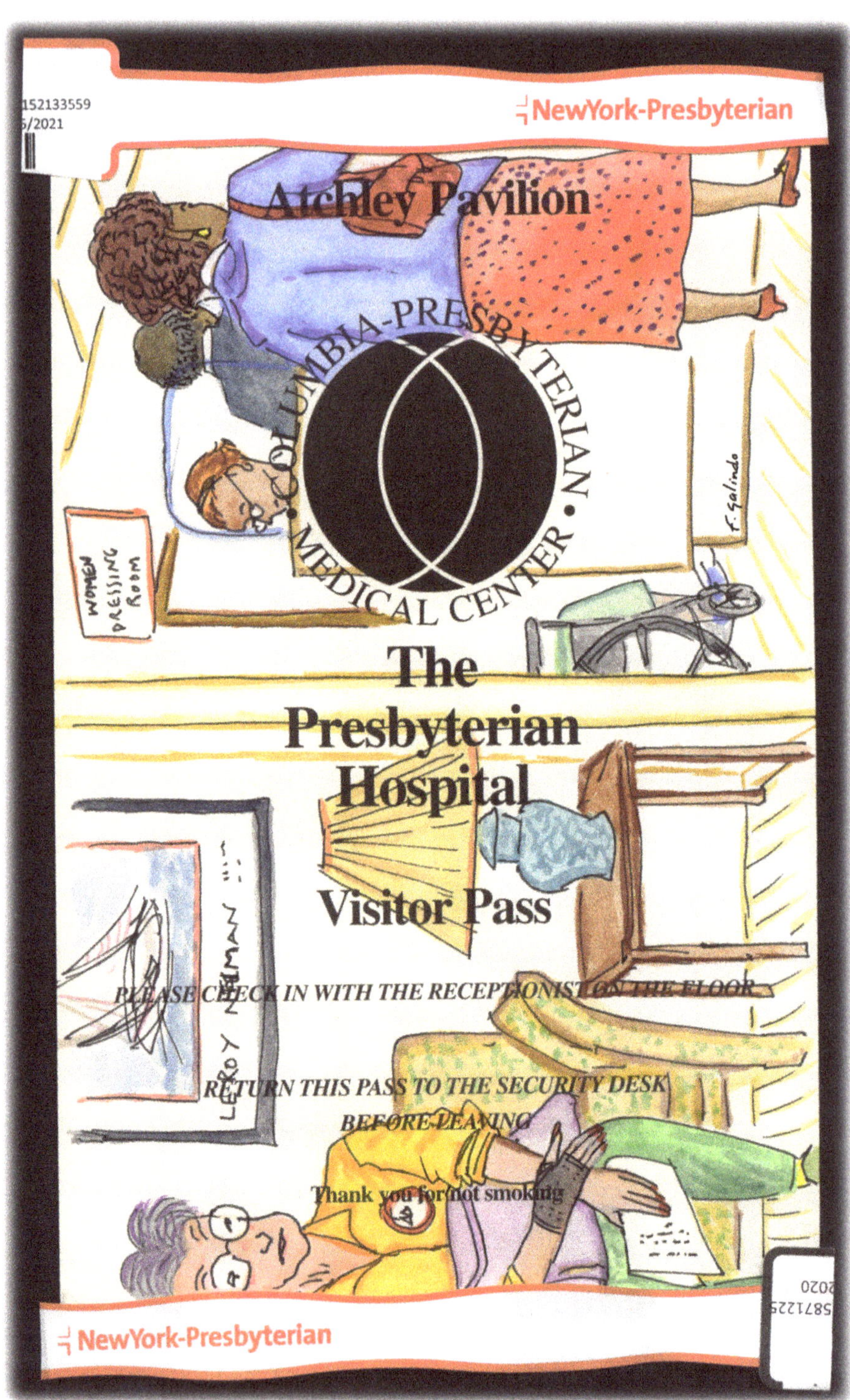
NewYork-Presbyterian
Atchley Pavilion
COLUMBIA-PRESBYTERIAN MEDICAL CENTER
The Presbyterian Hospital
Visitor Pass
PLEASE CHECK IN WITH THE RECEPTIONIST ON THE FLOOR
RETURN THIS PASS TO THE SECURITY DESK BEFORE LEAVING
Thank you for not smoking
WOMEN DRESSING ROOM
F. Galindo
NewYork-Presbyterian

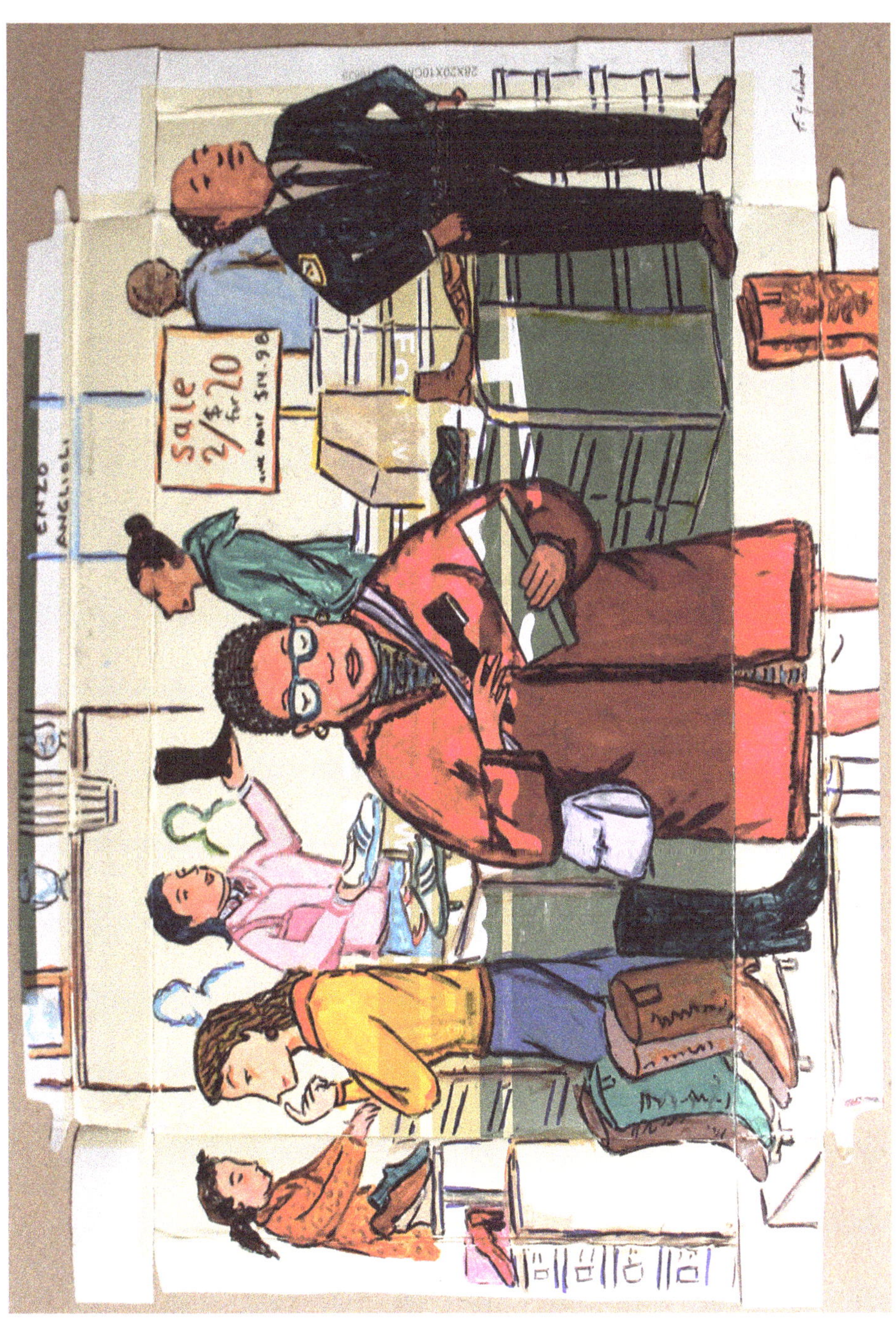
Sale
2/$ for 20

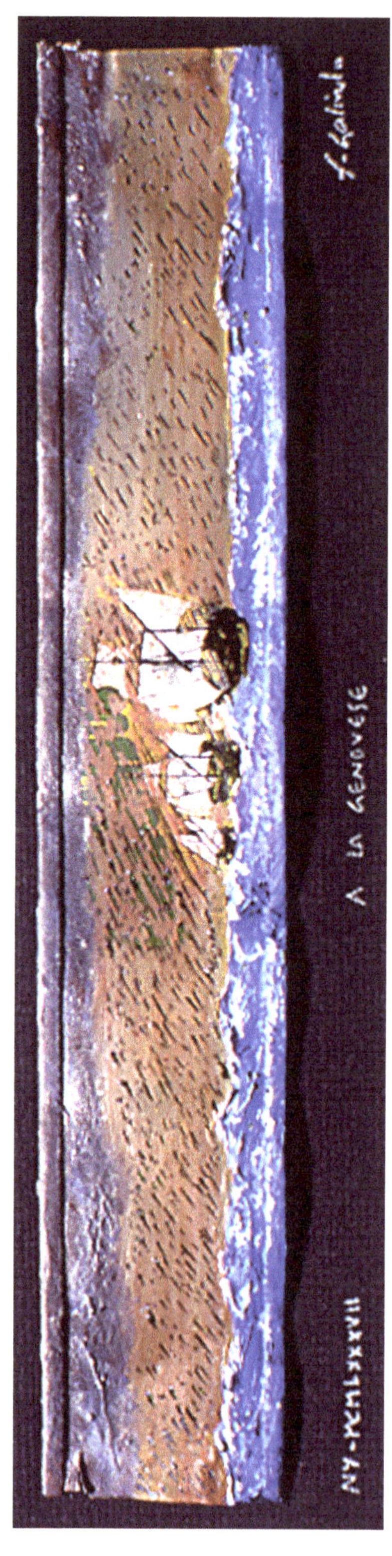
A LA GENOVESE
NY-MCMLXXXVII

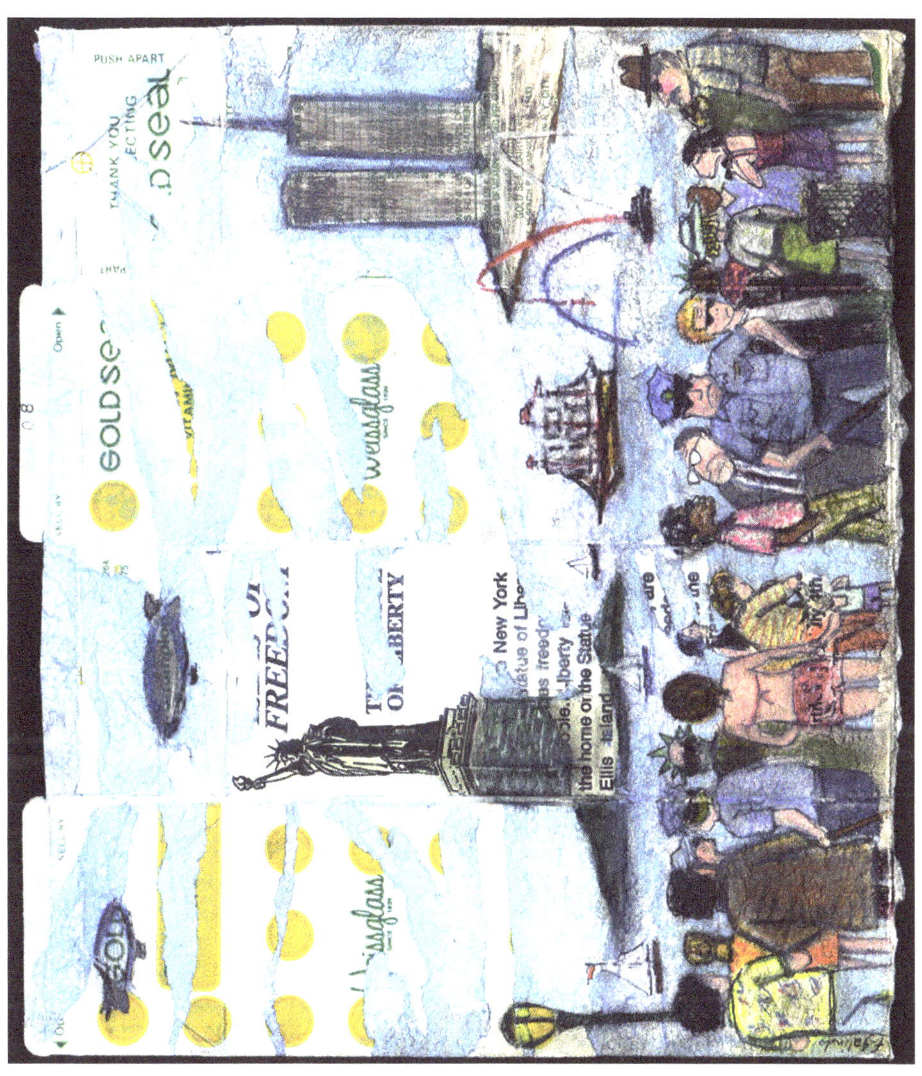
PUSH APART
THANK YOU
New York
the home of the Statue
Ellis Island

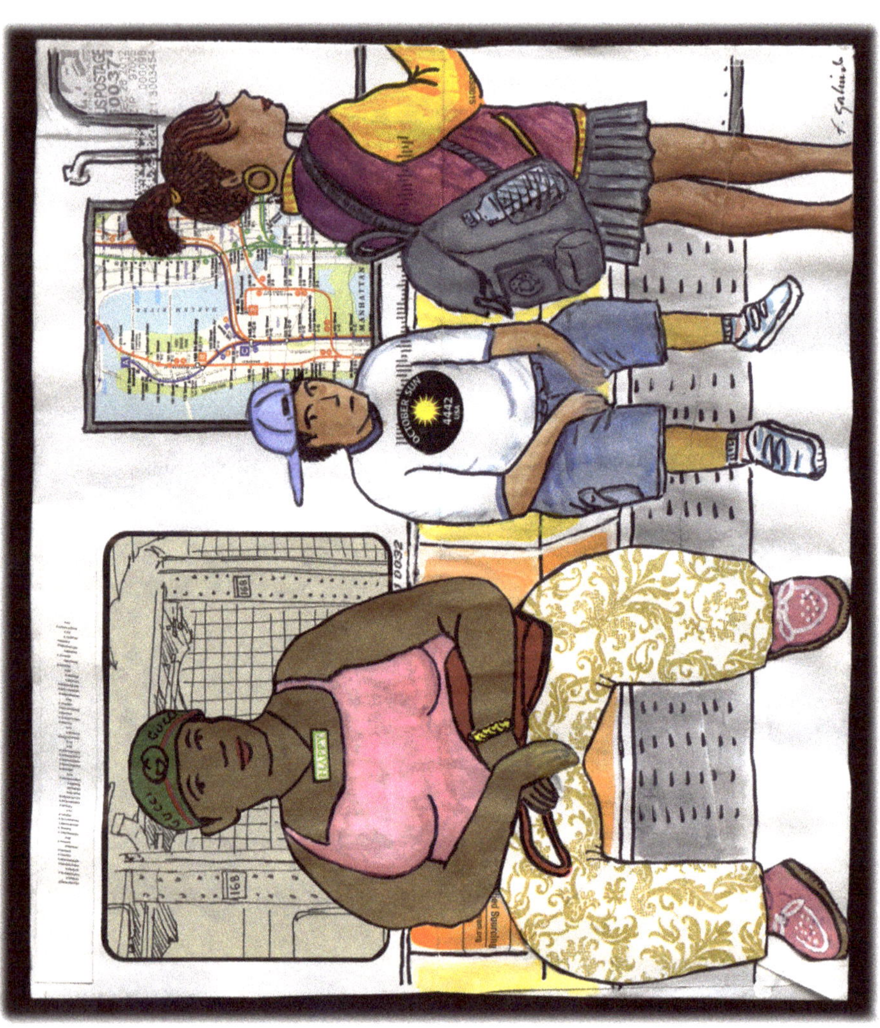
US POSTAGE
MANHATTAN
OCTOBER SUN
4442
USA

TOMPKINS SQ.
SANDWICHES · COFFEE
COLD BEER · SODA
DELI & GROCERY
Entenmann's
SINCE 1898
DELI
HOT & COLD SANDWICHES
BEER & SODA
DOS EQUIS
BEER
BUD
LIGHT
GENESEE
PECAN DANISH
RING
NET WT. 15 OZ.
$3.08 $2.89
OPEN HERE
LAST SALE DATE—SEE BOTTOM
DELICIOUS HEATED
IN MICROWAVE
ENTENMANN'S, INC. BAY SHORE, NY 11706
MIAMI, FL 33147, CHICAGO, IL 60164
MONTEBELLO, CA 90640
CT LIC 3119, REG. PENNA. DEPT OF AGR

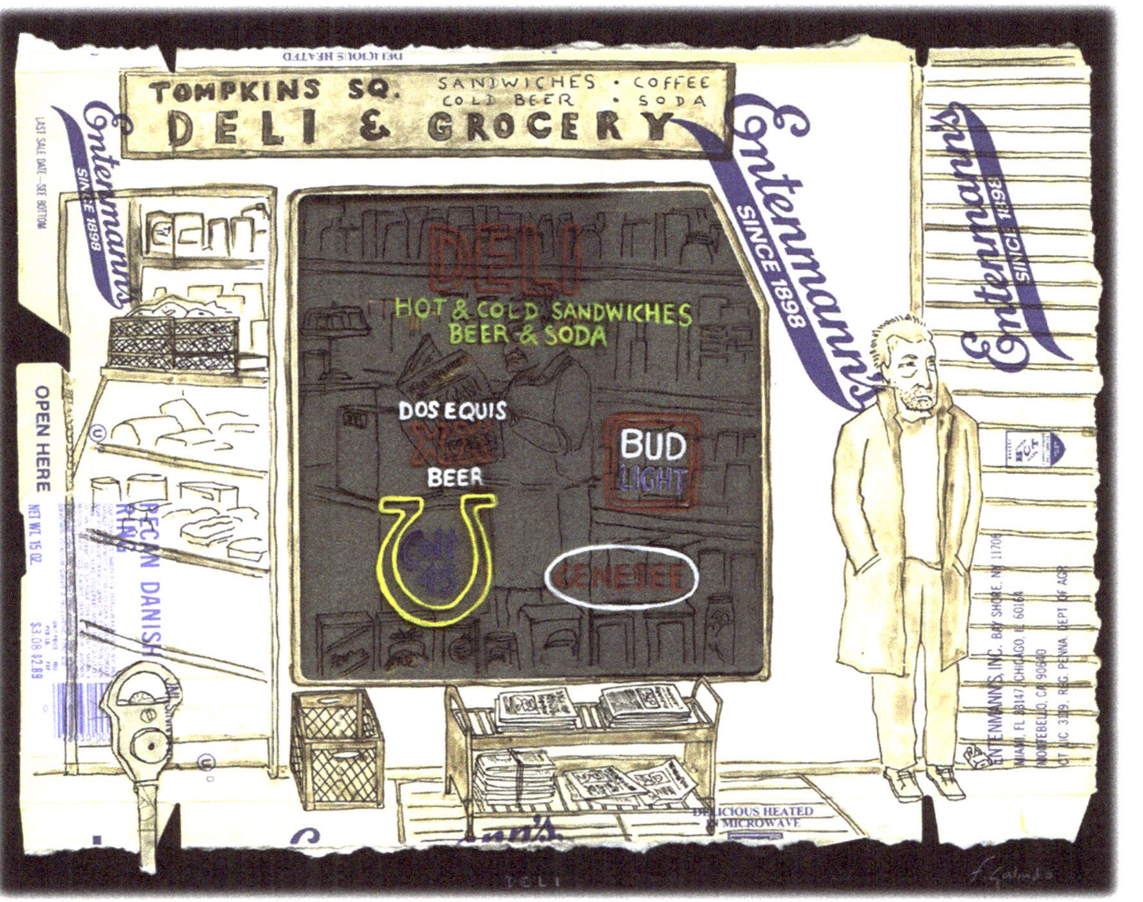

DELI

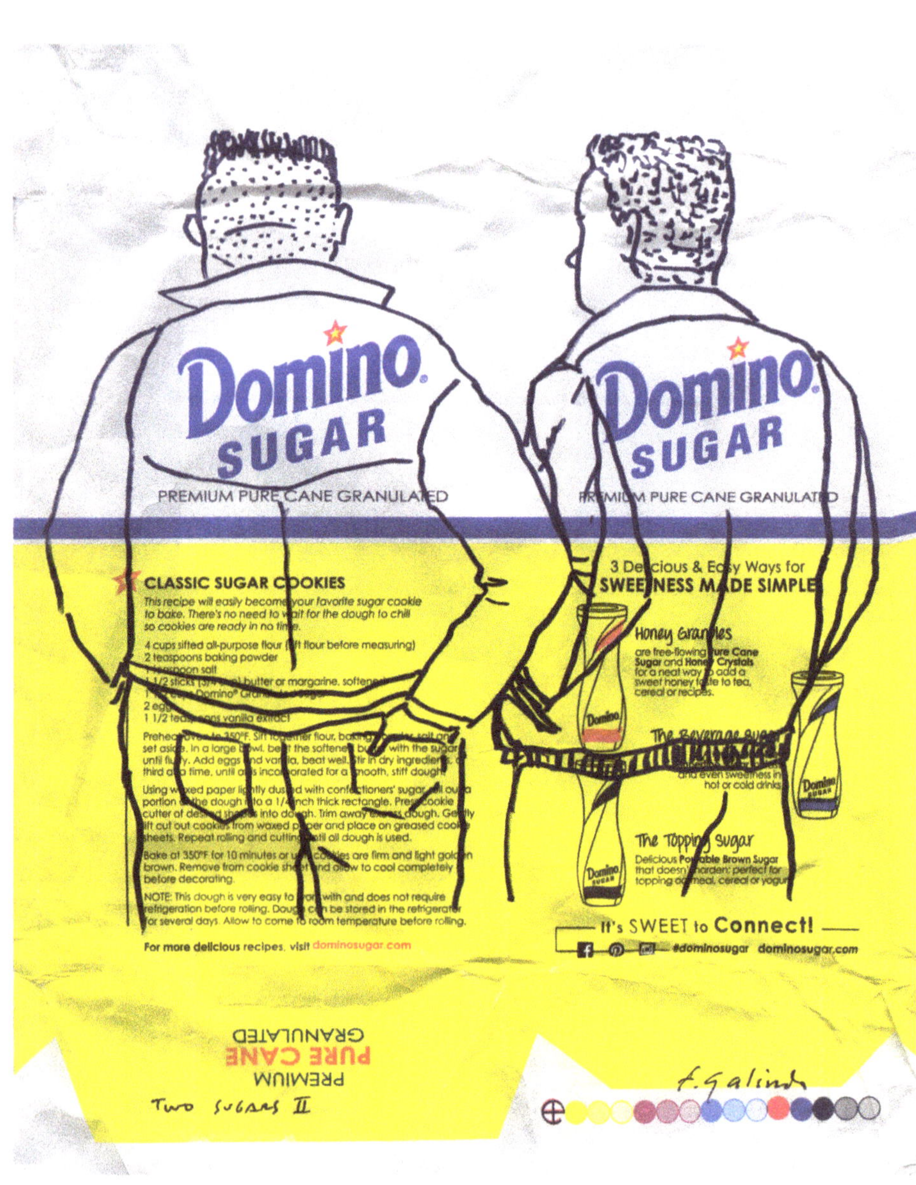
Domino
SUGAR
PREMIUM PURE CANE GRANULATED
Domino
SUGAR
CLASSIC SUGAR COOKIES
The Topping Sugar
It's SWEET to Connect!
#dominosugar dominosugar.com
For more delicious recipes, visit dominosugar.com
Two Sugars II
F. Galindo

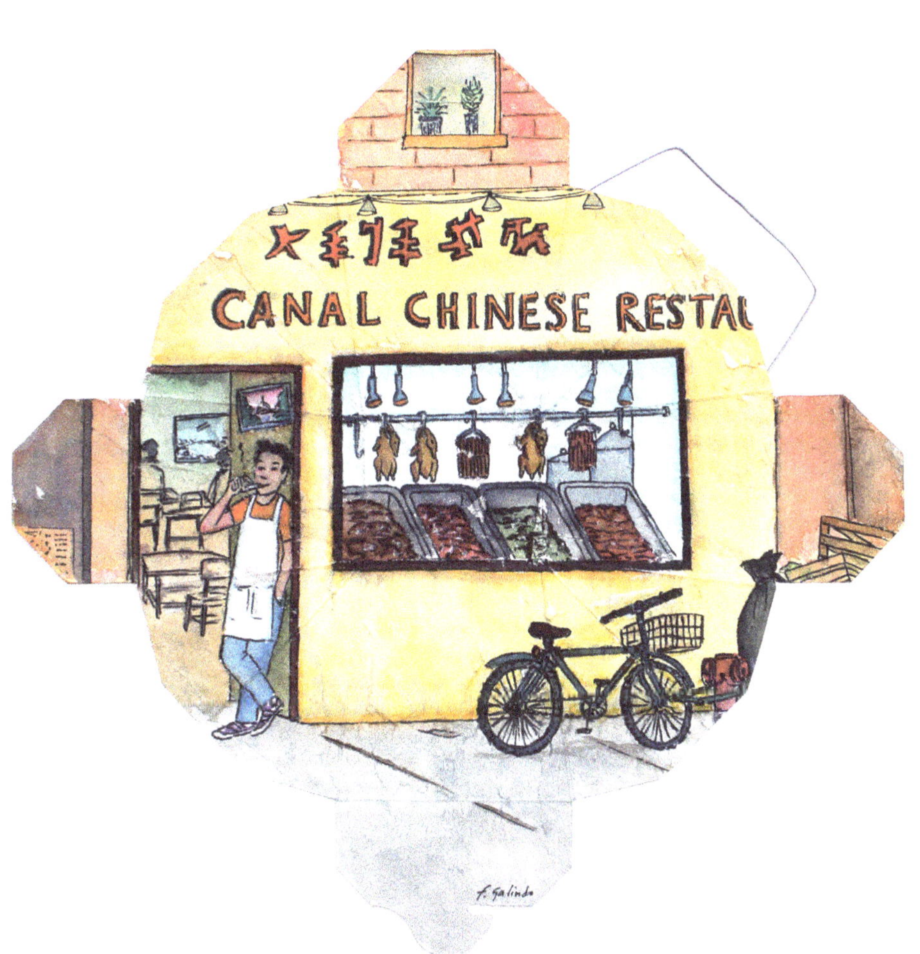
CANAL CHINESE RESTAU

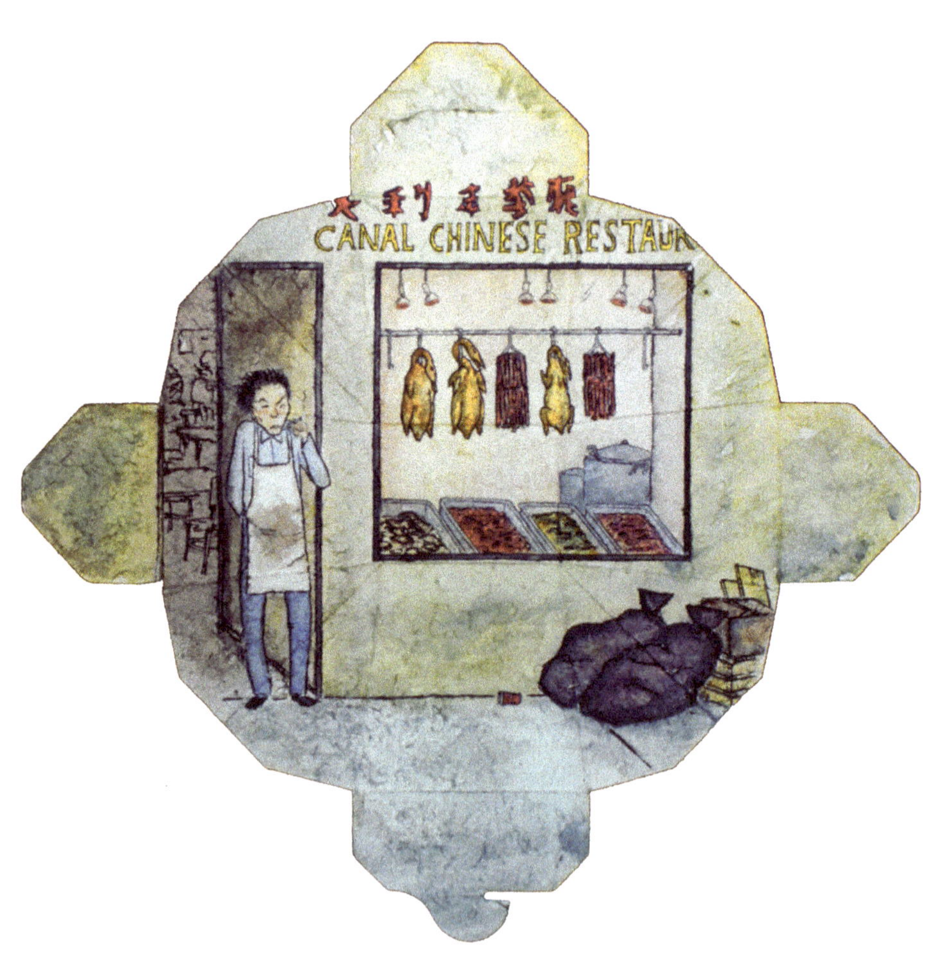
CANAL CHINESE RESTAUR

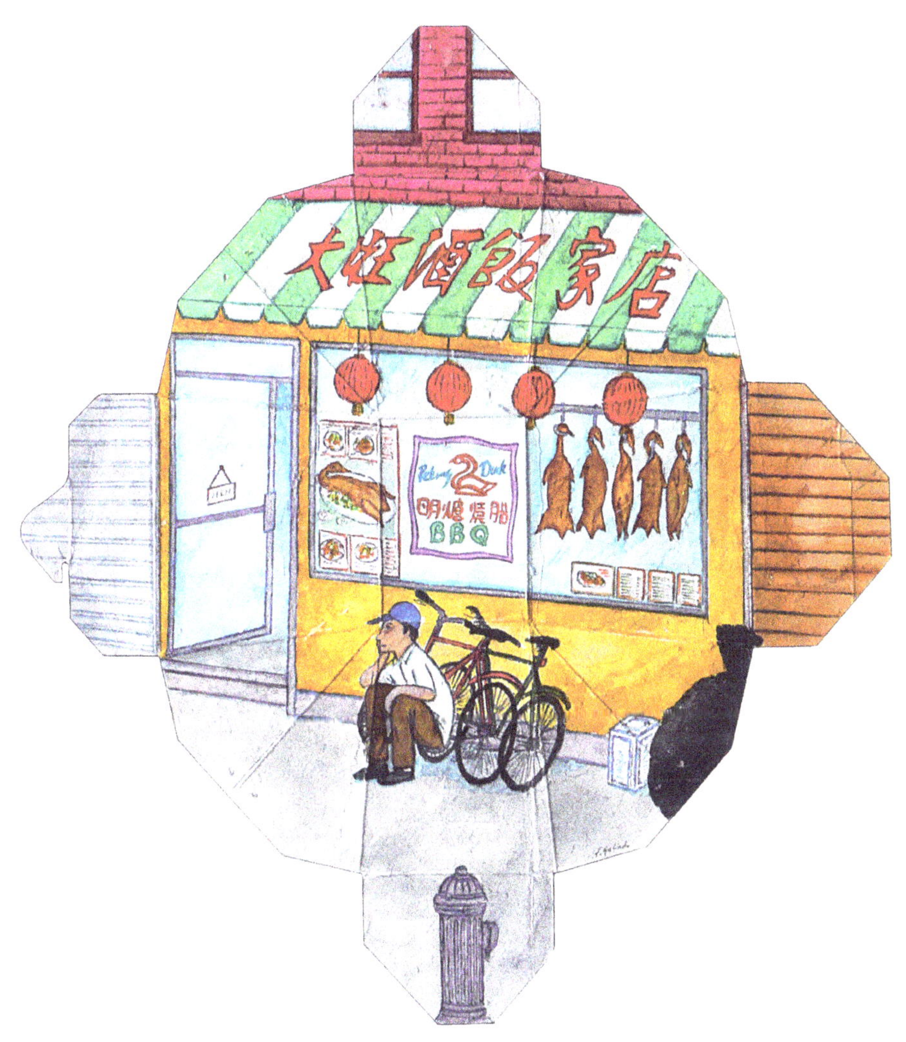
Duck
BBQ

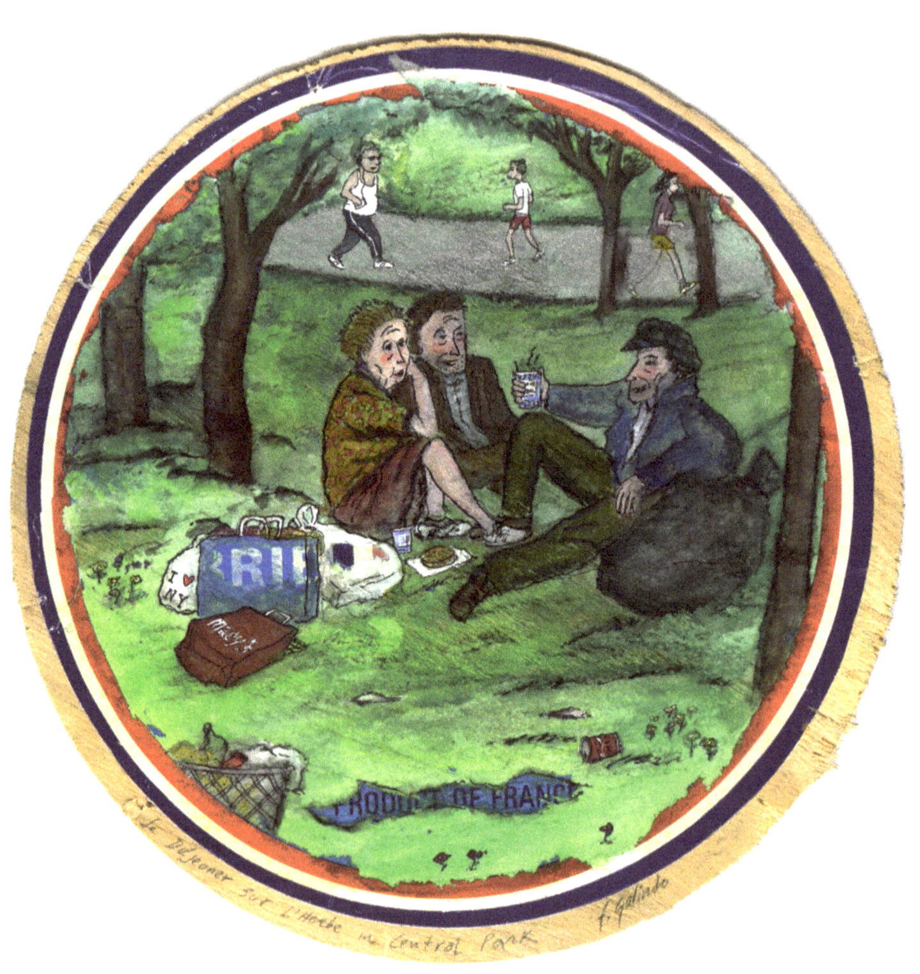
BRI
I ♥ NY
Macy's
OF FRANC
Le Dejeuner Sur L'Herbe in Central Park
F. Galindo

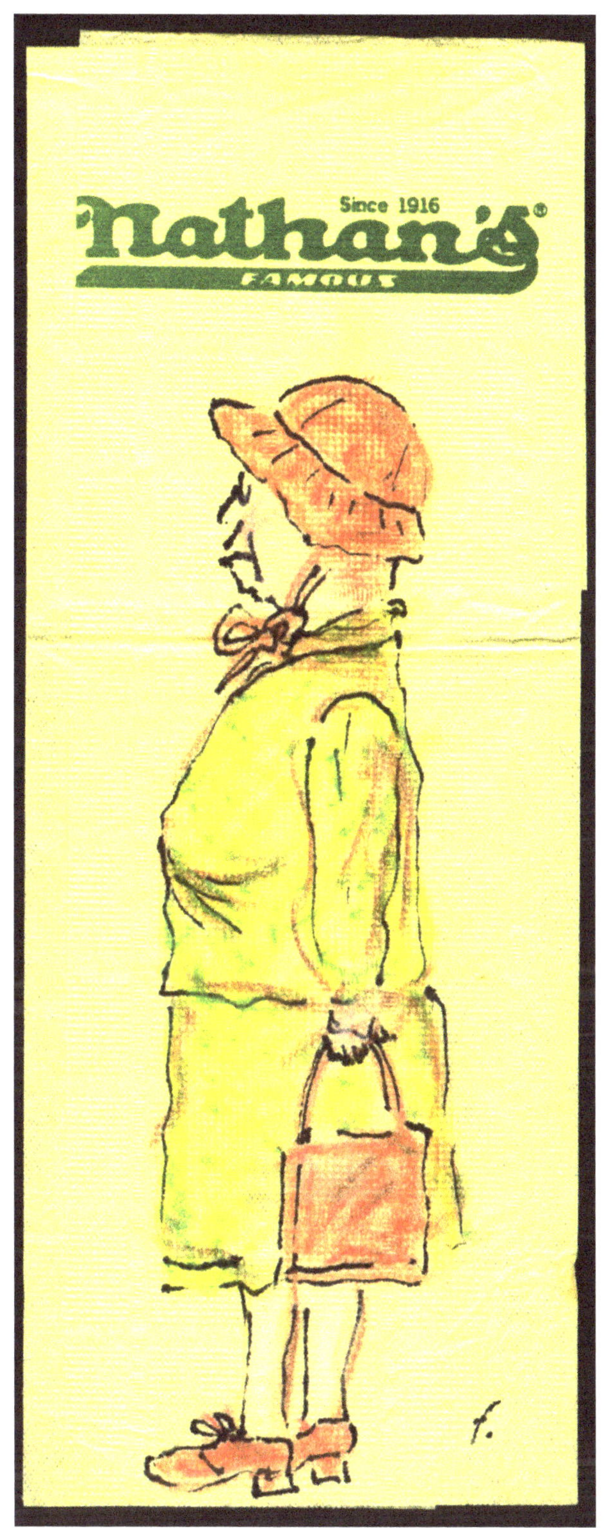
Since 1916
Nathan's®
FAMOUS

USED / REUSED
Artwork List

Page 6. *Coffee Shop I*, 11x14", ink & watercolor on paper & coffee cup. Jennifer Beals Collection.

Page 9. *The Sound of Music*, 3x5", ink & watercolor on concert ticket.

Page 11. *New Yorkers I*, 11x8.5", Mixed media on magazine paper wrapper. Private Collection.

Page 12. Sketches for *Subway Series VI* & *Duro*, ink on paper.

Page 13. *Subway Series VI* & *Duro*, 10x8" & 10 x 5", ink & watercolor on paper bag.

Page 14. *Bus Stop I*, 11x14", ink & pastel on bus transfers. Peter Schleger Collection.

Page 15. *Bus Stop II*, 11x14", ink & pastel on bus transfers. Private Collection.

Page 16. *Coney Island Horses*, 11x11", ink & watercolor on paper plate.

Page 17. *Coney Islanders I* (Private Collection) & *Coney Islanders II*, 10x5", ink, watercolor & pastel on paper bag.

Page 18. *McDonald's Ladies* & *Met Dining*, 10x5", ink & watercolor on paper bag.

Page 19. *Habitat*, 18x14", ink & watercolor on paper bag.

Page 20. *Ms. Brown* (Victoria Roberts Collection) & *Merry Xmas Mrs. Lawrence*, 10x5", ink & watercolor on paper bag.

Page 21. *Saks in the City*, 18x14", scratched paper bag.

Page 22. *Saints in the City II*, 18x14", ink, watercolor & pastel on paper with yogurt top.

Page 23. *Midnight Dragons*, 10x12", ink & acrylic on beer can. Private Collection.

Page 24. *Bud*, 10x12", ink & acrylic on beer can.

Page 25. *Buddies II* (Marymount College Collection) & *Buddies III*, (Suzy del Valle Collection) 10x12", ink & acrylic on beer can.

Page 26. *Andrei at Miss Brooks* & *Two Sugars I* (Peter Schleger Collection,) 1.5x2.25", ink & watercolor on sugar packet.

Page 27. *Venus de Milo*, 10x5", ink, watercolor & pastel on paper bag. Alison Loeb Collection.

Page 28. *Mc WaHi*, 12x10", ink & watercolor on takeout bag.

Page 29. *Guardian Angel* & *Mc Siesta*, 10x5" & 10x8", ink, watercolor & pastel on paper bags.

Page 30. *Coffee Shop III*, 11x14", ink & watercolor on paper & coffee cup. Private Collection.

Page 31. *Coffee Shop IV*, 11x14", ink & watercolor on paper & coffee cup. Private Collection.

Page 32. *Coffee Shop V*, 11x14", ink & watercolor on paper & coffee cup. Private Collection.

Page 33. *Coffee Shop VI*, 11x14", ink & watercolor on paper & coffee cup. Private Collection.

Page 34. *Coffee With a View*, 5x5", ink & watercolor on Danish pastry tray.

Page 35. *Yankees* (Mark Miller Collection) & *At The Met Café I & II*, 11x8.5", ink & watercolor on coffee cups.

Page 36. *Little Red Lighthouse*, 5x7", ink & watercolor on tree leaf.

Page 37. *Art Lovers IV*, 12x12", ink & watercolor on museum brochure.

Page 38. *Art Lovers I*, 20x8", ink & watercolor on museum brochure. Mark Miller Collection.

Page 39. *Art Lovers II*, 11x14", ink & watercolor on museum brochure. Carol Ward Collection.

Page 40. *Art Lovers III*, 10x8", ink & watercolor on museum brochure. Private Collection.

Page 41. *Art Lovers V: Philippe De Montebello Explains Goya*, 10x8", ink & watercolor on museum brochure. Private Collection.

Page 42. *Morning News*, 13x8", ink, watercolor on paper plate & plastic cutlery. Private Collection.

Page 43. *Lunch Break*, 13x8", ink, watercolor, acrylic on paper plate & plastic cutlery.

Page 44. *Lunchtime Landscape*, 11x14", mixed media on a paper menu & chopsticks. Private Collection.

Page 45. *To Stay Or To Go?*, 13x9", ink & watercolor on a paper menu & chopsticks.

Page 46. *The Bus Series I Detail* & *Sketch*, ink, watercolor & pastel on paper bus map.

Page 47. *The Bus Series I Detail* & *Sketch*, ink, watercolor & pastel on paper bus map.

Page 48. *The Bus Series II*, 13x36", ink, watercolor & pastel on paper bus map.

Page 49. *The Bus Series I*, 13x36", ink, watercolor & pastel on paper bus map. Private Collection.

Page 50. *The Bus Series III*, 11x8.5", ink & watercolor on magazine wrapping.

Page 51. *The Subway Series II*, 11x8.5", ink, watercolor & collage on magazine wrapping.

Page 52. *Readings* , 8x10", ink and watercolor on paper & *Saints in the City*, 8x10", ink & watercolor on paper with yogurt top. Private Collection.

Page 53. *The Subway Series III & IV* (Peter Schleger Collection,) 9x12", ink & watercolor on windowed envelope.

Page 54. *Underground*, 20x23", ink, watercolor & pastel on subway map. Private Collection.

Page 55. *The Subway Series I*, 20x23", ink, watercolor & pastel on subway map.

Page 56. *Underground Lady Sketch*, 10x8", ink on paper.

Page 57. *Underground Lady*, 23x30", ink, watercolor & pastel on subway map. Private Collection.

Page 58. *Aisle No. 2*, 9x11", Acrylic on styrofoam tray.

Page 59. *All Aboard*, 11x14", ink, watercolor & pastel on bus ticket sleeve.

Page 60. *At the Permanente Collection II*, 20x27", ink, watercolor & pastel on museum shopping bag. Private Collection.

Page 61. *At the Permanente Collection I*, 20x27", ink, watercolor & pastel on museum shopping bag. Sidney Harris Collection.

Page 62. *Waiting Room*, 8x10", watercolor and collage on hospital visitor pass.

Page 63. *Shoe Shopping*, 22x17", ink & acrylic on shoe box.

Page 64. *A la Genovese*, 11x2.5", acrylic on tin can. Patricia Vega Collection.

Page 65. *Fourth of July*, 11x8.5", ink, watercolor & acrylic on milk carton. Private Collection.

Page 66. *The Subway Series VI*, 9x11", ink, watercolor & collage on windowed envelope.

Page 67. *Deli*, 11x8.5", ink, watercolor & acrylic on cake box. Private Collection.

Page 68. *Two Sugars II*, 11x9", ink on paper sugar bag.

Page 69. *Roasted Ducks II*, 22x22", ink, watercolor & pastel on Chinese takeout box. Private Collection.

Page 70. *Roasted Ducks I*, 22x22", ink, watercolor & pastel on Chinese takeout box. A. Zentella Collection.

Page 71. *Roasted Ducks III*, 22x22", ink, watercolor & pastel on Chinese takeout box.

Page 72. *Le Déjeuner Sur L'herbe*, 12x12", ink, watercolor, pastel on wooden cheese box.

Page 73. *Nathan's Lady*, 8x3.5", ink on paper napkin.

ACKNOWLEDGMENTS

Dedicated to my muses Andrea Arroyo and New York City.

Special Thank You to the following persons and institutions:

Shiloh Holley, C. Stanley Ledbetter, Peter Schleger, Mark Miller, James Bacchi, Linh Dinh, Carol Ward, Rocío Alvarado, Jennifer Beals, Sid Harris, Victoria Roberts, Martin Kozlowski, Frank di Gregory, Sherry Mazzocchi, Alex Zentella, Scot W. Thompson, Fred & Irene Rosen, Patricia Vega, Corinne Myller, Upper Manhattan Empowerment Zone, Lower Manhattan Cultural Council, The Morris-Jumel Mansion.

And to departed friends: Wes Anderson, Vivien Raynor, Holly Block.

Artworks on this book have been exhibited in New York City at:

On The Wall Gallery; PS 122 Gallery; Art In General; The New Yorker Gallery; El Museo del Barrio (S) Files Biennal at Lehman College, Bronx and Rotunda Gallery, Brooklyn; The Bronx Museum; Mark Miller Gallery; PhilosophyBox Gallery; El Taller Latinoamericano; The Interchurch Center; Marymount Manhattan College Art Gallery; Krasdale Foods Art Gallery; Henry Street Settlement; Bronx Blue Bedroom Project; North of History Gallery; Rio II Gallery; Clemente Soto Velez Cultural Center; NoMAA Gallery; Sikkema Jenkins & Co.; NYFA Art Gallery; Governors Island Art Fair; The Alternative Museum; Chashama West Village.

And also at: The Montclaire State University Art Gallery, NJ.; Long Island Brentwood Gallery, NY.; New Arts Program Gallery, PA.; The Brevard Art Museum, FL.; Hopper House Gallery, Nyack, NY.

Other Books by Felipe Galindo Feggo

Manhatitlan: Mexican and American Cultures Intertwined (J. Pinto Books)

No Man Is a Desert Island (J. Pinto Books)

Cats Will Be Cats (Plume/Penguin)

George Washington: Back in New York City (Now What Media

Taking Liberties (Now What Media)

Other Now What Books

Silver Linings Plague Book

Gertrude et Alice

Trump Tweets Alt-American History

Talk to the Hair

Flick and Flak: More Poison Capsule Reviews

The Golem's Voice

Further Adventures: Now What Anthology No. 1

PK in the Terrarium

Downtown Drowned

The Da Vinci Cold

Go the Fk Back to Work!**

Fairly Grim Tales

Love the Sinner, Hate the Cinema

Gertrude's Follies

INX Battle Lines: Three Decades of Political Illustration

www.ingramcontent.com/pod-product-compliance
Lightning Source LLC
LaVergne TN
LVHW052348100826
845147LV00012B/783

* 9 7 8 0 9 9 6 2 3 6 6 8 3 *